NATIVE AMERICAN MOCCASINS

A Craft Manual

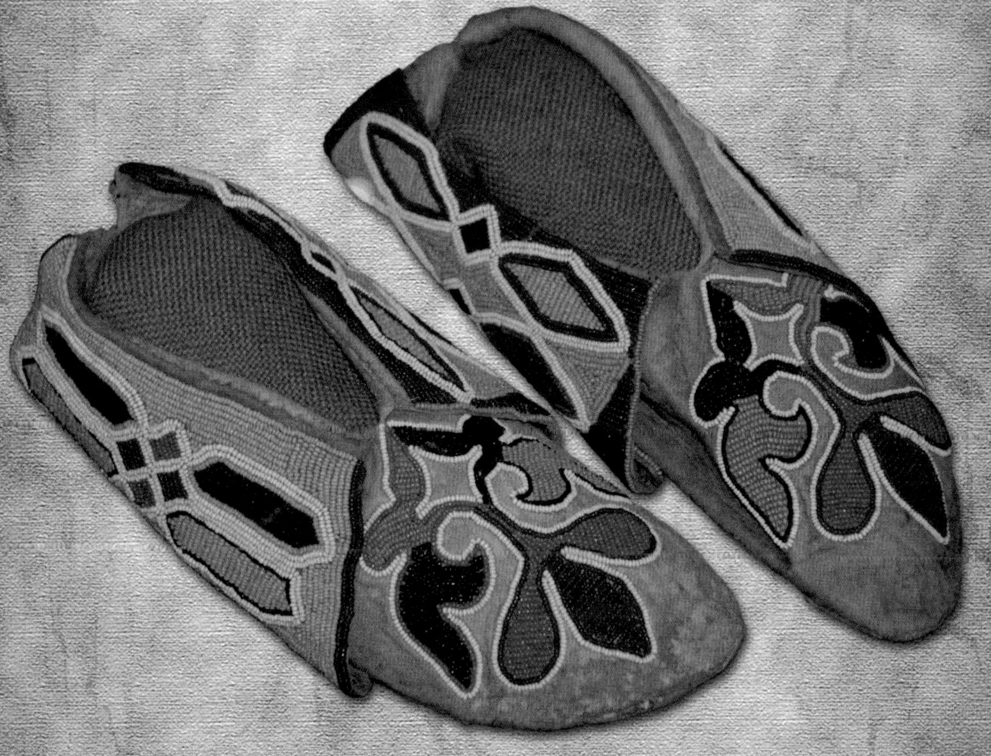

by George M. White

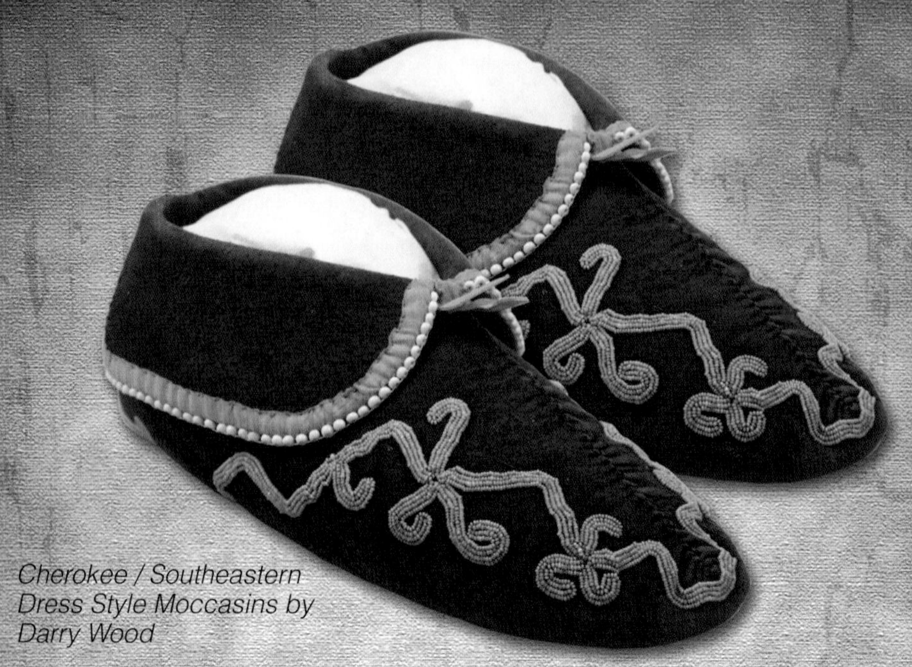

Cherokee / Southeastern Dress Style Moccasins by Darry Wood

Published by
Crazy Crow Trading Post, LLC
Box 847
Pottsboro, TX 75076
www.crazycrow.com

First Edition: January, 1969
Second Edition: January, 1992
Third Edition: December, 2013

Edited by: J. Rex Reddick and Barry E. Hardin
Design by: Michael Catellier and J.Rex Reddick
Illustrations by: the Author and Ed Wells

ISBN: 1-929572-26-3

Acknowedgements

We would like to thank the following individuals and institutions for their help in providing photographs and information. Darry Wood, Earl Fenner, Ginger Reddick, Richard Green, Jim Cooley, Joe Rosenthal, Adam Lovell of the Detroit Historical Society, Suzanne McClean of the Bata Shoe Museum, Barry Landua of the American Museum of Natural History, Henry Monahan of Morning Star Gallery and Delia Sullivan of Heritage Auctions.

ABOUT THE AUTHOR

JAMES V. REYES-PICKNELL is a recognized authority in maintenance and asset management and the founder of Conscious Asset, a consulting and training firm that helps asset-intensive organizations improve performance through better decision-making, governance, and execution.

A Certified Management Consultant (CMC) and Professional Engineer, James has worked globally across a wide range of industries, including mining, manufacturing, energy, transportation, natural resources, pharmaceuticals, healthcare, and public infrastructure. He is frequently sought out by leading consulting firms and organizations for his deep expertise in reliability and asset management.

His career spans hands-on engineering roles, senior leadership positions, and decades of advisory work with organizations seeking to move beyond reactive maintenance toward reliable, value-driven asset performance.

James is widely known for his work on the Uptime framework, originally introduced by John Dixon Campbell in 1995. As co-author of subsequent editions, he has helped evolve Uptime into a practical systems model integrating leadership, work management, reliability, information, and governance. In *Steadfast*, he extends that evolution further, positioning maintenance and reliability as strategic enablers of organizational performance and long-term value creation.

He has taught maintenance and asset management in university and professional programs, contributed to industry standards discussions, and published extensively in leading journals. His work emphasizes that sustainable performance is achieved not through tools alone, but through aligned systems, disciplined thinking, and leadership that recognize both the technical and human dimensions of reliability.

Table of Contents

About this Revised Edtion

When it comes to examining material culture items from Native Americans, nothing seems so personal as a pair of moccasins. Perhaps this is because each pair was made to fit the feet of a particular individual and, thus, becomes more identifiable with a specific human being who once wore them while treading Mother Earth.

The construction of the moccasins also speaks to the tribal culture to which the wearer belonged.

In 1915, the renowned anthropologist, Clark Wissler, undertook an analysis of various articles of Native American clothing in an effort to compare or contrast basic construction traits. In so doing, he arrived at the following conclusion: "… it is clear that scarcely a single important feature of a given garment is peculiar to a single tribe but that two or more in geographical continuity share it equally." In other words, tribes that lived in the same geographic area were likely to have garment items with shared construction patterns and techniques. If we relate this to moccasins, we find that tribes in the same locale were likely to have moccasins constructed in the same manner. Tribal distinctions more likely arrive upon examining the decorations, such as beadwork. However, beadwork/quillwork techniques and designs also often overlap into neighboring tribes, so that tribal identification by looking at beadwork is not necessarily an exact science.

For those who wish to reproduce moccasins of a specific tribal style, it is important to research printed and on-line sources in an effort to learn (1) how were that tribe's moccasins made during a certain time period, and (2) how were they decorated during that particular period? Problems arise, however, from the facts that, for some tribes, there are few – if any – collected specimens, and, unfortunately, many specimens are misidentified. Museums and printed texts, regrettably, often display Native American garment items that are incorrectly identified as to tribal attribution and date of manufacture. This often is the result of poor or absent field notes from when the article was collected. For the would-be craftsman, these misidentifications often lead to confusion. However, after looking at many specimens, it often is possible to discern consistent construction traits, and this information can then be used to determine what moccasin style, at least, would be representative of a particular tribe at a particular time.

As inferred from Wissler's study, even if we can find no collected examples from a particular tribe, by researching moccasins from neighboring tribes, we often can discover styles that were common to tribes who shared the same geographic region. And so it follows that we reasonably can assume that our target tribe had the same style.

With this knowledge in hand, we hope that this book, Native American Moccasins – A Craft Manual, will help craftsmen recreate moccasins for their particular purpose. Even if the book does not present moccasin construction for the specific tribe in which you are interested, you will probably find a similar style used by a neighboring tribe.

Barry E. Hardin and J. Rex Reddick
Crazy Crow Trading Post, LLC
November, 2013

Introduction

The word "moccasin" just happened because the Algonquin people along the New England coast told the first white settlers the name of their footwear. The word has since been used to identify the leather footwear of most of the Indian people of North America.

Most of the moccasins were made of soft tanned leather; there are some exceptions, but for the most part the tanning process was basically the same with all peoples. The flesh-ing (removing all tissue, fats and flesh on the inside of the hide) was necessary in all cases. Hair was removed or left on, depending on its intended use. If hair was to be removed, the standard method was to chop or scrape the hair off. This method always removed the outer "grain" of the leather, producing the suede look of all Indian tanned leather. Various meth-ods were used to "break down" and soften the leather. One ingredient was always there and that was hard manual labor. The softened leather was white and often left that way by some Plains people, but for the most part it seems all woodland people preferred to smoke their leather as this aided in the tanning and service of the leather. The smoking produced a brownish leather which withstood moisture better than the white leather.

Moccasins were found in all North America except south of the border in Mexico and the northern fringe where Eskimo cultures prevail. This is, of course, only a broad statement with exceptions.

As we study moccasins, several points of interest appear. We might become curious about distribution of a particular type or why a certain type is found in a certain location, or we might wonder as to how long it took to perfect the footwear we see today.

As for time, the archeologist and other specialists tell us that it would have been possible for early man to have made footwear seventy-five thousand years ago. The last Great Ice Age would have forced many northern hunters to perfect a protective covering for his body and may have caused people to migrate onto the North American continent. It is fairly well agreed that man has been on this continent twenty-thousand years. The remains of his cul-ture are comparable to the culture of Europe of the same period. The remains are necessar-ily stone implements as organic materials have small chance of surviving so great a time.

There are at least two reasons why we think this early North American had footwear. First, the stone artifacts of his culture indicate he was intelligent enough to produce leather goods. Secondly, if he had come to this land by the northern route, from Asia to Alaska, then it would seem most necessary that he had some protection for his body and feet.

Twenty-thousand years ago the Great Continental Glacier must have sprawled over the en-tire land mass of Canada and pushed into the United States. Thousands of Alpine Glaciers spewed ice and frigid waters into mountain valleys from Alaska to California. There may have been ice free corridors running north and south that would provide passage as well as plants and animals for food.

The distribution of moccasin types also offers food for thought. We assume that we have twenty-thousand years to consider distribution and movement of people and also the same time for perfection of design. We must consider some limitation as to ways leather can be manipulated to produce footwear. The "Center Seam" as a basic design seems to have the greatest distribution and is the most predominant design. The "Gathered Toe", "Side Seam", Two Piece" (a hard sole and soft sole), and "Shaped Sole" fall into smaller areas of less distribution. This distribution seems to indicate a possible inter-play of cultures and people in an arc south of the Great Lakes to Maine and perhaps along the southern fringe of the ice mass.

A series of designs show up in this area while north of this line a predominant type (a modified center seam) moves north to the Arctic following the retreat of the ice. South of this line a true center seam prevails. In a Southwest section joining this line, a third modified center seam (see Winnebago) is found. Closely related in the same area is found a side seam type which also appears in the Western Rocky Mountain areas.

The "Two-Piece" hard sole appears as a modification on the high, dry Plains in the West. Several things indicate that this "Hard Sole" moccasin was a product of the high Plains as a must rather than a choice. The hard sole was harder to make than the soft sole, but it gave greater protection from cactus and hard prairie ground.

The last moccasin to be considered is the Apache and Navajo. We are told that these people were the last group to move down from the north. The moccasin study also indicates this as there is strong resemblance in design of the Apache / Navajo footwear to the Northern Indian and Eskimo Mukluk. This moccasin group will be called the "shaped Sole" type. It would seem to suggest that these people moved from the north rather quickly and retained their footwear designs and found them as well suited to the harsh desert and plains as they were to the northern ice.

The Apache also retained an odd shaped sole design that has distinct "Mongolian" characteristics. The lifted, pointed toe is also suggestive of Lapp footwear. Many North American Indian moccasins show characteristics of Asian footwear, but as mentioned before there are limited ways in which leather can be manipulated and it is possible many different groups could have developed similar designs.

The time element and designs development can only be projected from bits of information and close examination and study or moccasins. This examination reveals a degree of perfection, considering the use of leather, tools and materials available, and the final product. This we choose to call "Climax Design", where there is little or no way to improve a particular moccasin's construction. Most moccasins show this "Climax Design", which must not be confused with transitional or "break-down" periods when the Indian economy was disrupted or destroyed by European advances.

Bits of information such as nine thousand year old sandals show sophistication and skill of that time; the needle of bone, dated thirteen thousand years; the Julian Steward Moccasin Collection dated eight hundred to nine hundred years ago, revealing "Climax Designs" equal or superior to a comparable moccasin found in the Yukon today. These tend to indicate the age of moccasin designs. The designs shown in this book could be from one thousand to ten thousand years old. The center seam type might even be older than ten thousand years. The main types of moccasins are shown in this book; however, there are many variations of these types which are not illustrated.

George M. White
1969

Introduction To Rawhide, Buckskin & Leather

By G. D. Wood

The preparation of skins, as it was done by most North American tribal people, results in two products that are substantially different from what most folks nowadays think of as "leather." The title of this essay is trying to make that point.

If the skin from an animal is not given human attention, it either freezes or rots away or dries out shriveled and hard, in any case not very useful. People all over the planet have discovered ways of preserving skins for practical use, which we call the art of tanning. This activity is named for the acidic compounds known as tannins, which are found in a great variety of plants. From this we get references to "bark tanning" and "vegetable tanning," which along with other naturally occurring acids and salts, form the basis of many ancient methods.

Most of the leathers we are familiar with come out of the European tradition of this salt-and-acid method. In modern times, vegetable tanning has largely been replaced by stronger chemical compounds that usually don't occur in nature. These produce leather that is better adapted to a commercial process because very little human manipulation is required. Whether we are involved with the harder, stiffer material in our belts, boots and saddles, or the softer, supple skins used for our gloves, suede jackets, etc., the fibers stay flexible because the natural glue from the animal has been chemically neutralized. This is true as well for furs or pelts, which form a category of tannage slightly distinct from leather.

A skin is no problem for an animal to live in because of a thick liquid medium that flows within the network of fibers and allows it to move and stretch. The substance is called by various names -- mucus, ground substance, "the glue", etc. This sticky fluid becomes the vehicle by which a dead skin dries naturally to a hardness similar to wood. The purpose of a tanning agent is to overcome this glue and thereby help the dried skin to stay relaxed.

Rather than preventing fiber lock-down with a chemical attack, a different tanning strategy is to displace some of the mucus with oils. Many kinds of animal fats, from egg yolks to fish oil, have been used for this purpose. The idea is that by working a lubricant into the fibers and then manipulating the skin as it dries, these billions of tiny strands slip and slide quickly across each other so that "the glue" can't grab hold and stick them together.

This is considered to be a physical change, rather than a chemical one. Some versions of this "oil tanning" process don't really produce much of a soft hide, and in some cases the results are quite greasy. It can be especially unpleasant when the fats become rancid and oil tanned skins start to fall apart, indicating there is also a chemical reaction going on there, but one that is more in the service of decay than preservation.

The essential procedure in preserving any animal skin is to remove the fat and flesh. Cleaning up the inside surface is called fleshing, despite wise guys wanting to point out it is de-fleshing that is really going on. Once this step is done, the skin can be dried; if kept in this condition, it will last indefinitely, no tanning agent required. The issue now is that for the resulting stiff skin to be easily stored or of any use, it needs to be held in tension as it dries and shrinks, so that once the glue sets up it will at least lie flat.

Has this hard sheet of material become leather yet? It all depends on how you want to define the term. Some people would say that at this point the hide is cured, but I shy away from that word because it is used to mean so many different things. The terminology widely agreed upon is that the skin in this state is no longer green, but it is still raw.

Rawhide is the term for stiff leather, Indian style, and it is rather straight-forward to make. The fleshy tissue is removed, the hair is scraped off and the skin is stretched and dried, not necessarily in that order. Buffalo rawhide, to cite the most notable example, was customarily dried before it was scraped. Rawhide was put to untold dozens of uses in traditional culture, the most iconic of these being shields, drumheads, knife sheaths, storage containers and cases of all kinds and, most pertinent to the subject of this book, moccasin soles.

Good quality rawhide is often whitened and made more flexible by working it a bit, but to turn it into something truly soft -- there is no better way to say this -- it takes brains.

Brain tanning, the very idea of it, strikes some people as so bizarre they cannot imagine how such a thing could have ever been "invented." But it's not too big a stretch to speculate that the basic phenomenon might have been independently discovered again and again, if we consider that hunter-gatherer societies tend to regard an animal's brain as a rich and precious food –what today we would call very high protein. Remember also that early nomadic people would have made food storage containers out of raw hide. When some stone-age mama unpacked a particularly nice dinner she was saving from a recent kill, I don't think it would have escaped her notice that the wrapper wanted to go soft.

Brain tissue contains oily proteins that provide the lubrication, which combined with a lot of pulling and stretching, makes possible a most wonderful physical change. These oils are emulsified, which means they combine readily with water. This gives us a lubricant so subtle that it's hard to recognize it is there, other than that the skin on your hands has a silky feel after handling brains.

Brains are always thoroughly mashed and then used in various consistencies, from a thick paste to a thin solution. Although raw brains alone will work fine, some tanners prefer to cook them, and others will make a mixture that might include grosser fats, liver, soaps and more. A grained hide can be made very soft using only eggs, so "brain-tan" is really a problematic term for describing Indian-style buckskin: not only can it be made with agents other than brains; by some definitions this physical approach to skin-softening is not really tanning at all.

Regardless of whether using pure brains or a combination of other substances, good buckskin is never rancid or greasy. In fact, it is potentially the lightest, driest, softest, fluffiest, warmest, strongest, best smelling, most washable "leather" you will ever touch or see.

It is beyond the scope of this introduction to discuss the tools and techniques of buckskin making, which are many and varied, and now are easier than ever to learn about. The goal here is to name a few of the defining attributes of this traditional material that make it an ideal fabric for moccasins and other garments. I do this in the hope that serious devotees of Native American arts will want to become well-acquainted with real buckskin.

All of the footwear styles shown in this book were developed using brain-tanned buckskin. That term has come into common use in only the last 40 years. Prior to the early 1970's, this unique form of leather was exclusively referred to as "Indian-tan". Even this term is probably not extremely old, since in the colonial era almost everybody made and used buckskin. The word has come to signify a process, one that applies well beyond a product from the male deer.

All buckskin is not equal. Three independent factors will contribute to the finished skin. First is the inherent quality that the animal brings: species characteristics, individual genetic traits and size, thickness variations, scars from wounds or parasites, etc. Then there is the damage, or lack of it, caused by those who killed and skinned the critter. Last, there is the skill and care imparted by the one who does the tanning. All things being equal, a brain-tanned deerskin will be stronger, softer, easier to sew, and longer lasting than if it were chemically tanned. And that says nothing about the way it performs and feels against the human body.

Buckskin breathes. It is pleasant to wear in warm weather, wicking away sweat and quickly drying. The loose fiber network insulates against the cold without allowing the wind to blow through. Soaking wet, it is slippery and soggy, not warm as wool but more so than linen or cotton. One of its great advantages over any textile is the way it moves through the bushes without snagging or picking up lots of burrs. The stuff is tough; moderately thick hides will wear like iron for many years.

By comparison, acid tannage is vulnerable to the alkalinity in perspiration and soaps. Clothing made from these skins deteriorates noticeably from being repeatedly sweated up and washed. This is likely to happen, because such leather does not breathe; it is hot and heavy in warm weather. The chromium-based salts that are standard in modern tanneries produce a skin that in cool weather feels cold and very inorganic. Plus, it weighs somewhat more per square foot than one would prefer. A most excellent, brain tanning California bush hippy once told me, “We like our heavy metals in our music, not in our hides”.

Buckskin is naturally snow white, and sometimes is used like that. But woe to the owner if the thing gets wet, because that wicked glue, that dratted snot, is lurking down amongst those very natural fibers. A lot of this substance has been wrung out and washed away, but there is still plenty of it in there, waiting, ready to seize up and turn a nice soft item into a large, crinkled-up booger. What makes buckskin unique is the final step of the process that gives it color and, more importantly, protects it against water by preventing it from returning to rawhide. We are now entering a realm where “getting smoked” is a very positive development.

Smoking does not waterproof buckskin, which by its very nature is always going to be absorbent. IF you want water repellency, get an oily, acid-tan leather with the grain on it. What smoking does is to condition the skin, so that when it dries out it will fluff back up again. Buckskin is usually smoked on both sides, but it is essential to do it on at least one, until a bit of yellow/brown can be seen lightly showing through on the other.

With furs and robes with hair on, one side is all you can do. As with the application of brains, all smoke penetration must be gotten entirely through the flesh surface.

Even a small amount of smoke goes a long way to permanently unlock nature’s code. Resins in the smoke are drawn in between the fibers and form a coating that discourages them from sticking together. Smoke gives the skin some additional body, as well as color. This is generally good, since one of the few complaints that can be heard about buckskin is that it is too supple for many purposes. The heat from the smoking fire assists in the break-down of molecular linkages between cells, which helps to maintain long-term softness, after much of the actual smoke has washed out.

A big challenge at this stage is to arrange the skin over a very low fire and to attend it with great care, so as to not accidentally scorch all that good work. Buckskin is largely composed of protein; just like our living skins, it will easily cook. It is wise to not let the rising smoke get the tannage any hotter than the temperature a person’s body can stand.

The length of time a skin needs to smoke can vary wildly, depending on the efficiency of the set-up, the type of vegetation burned, the color desired, wind conditions, etc.

By taking the time to get a moderately strong smoke on both sides, the buckskin's softness seems to hold up better over time. The color will noticeably fade after washing, but the flexibility of the garment will bounce back with a bit of pulling and rubbing, although fringes will never be as pretty as new. Freshly smoked buckskin can be quite strong-smelling and slightly sticky, so some artists prefer to wash the entire thing before they begin to cut, sew or decorate. This makes it more pleasant to work with and also ensures that the skin will return to its true shape, which sometimes becomes distorted in the stretching and drying phase.

Always hand-wash buckskins; use a very small amount of soft soap and only luke-warm water. Rinse and wring gently, the way you would a fine piece of woolen, then block it out in the shade on a towel or blanket. Catch it when the piece is turning from slightly damp to all-but-dry (the same exact moment before the raw buckskin was originally "made") and all it will take is a few shakes to render it soft again. This is the perfect time to put on the dress, shirt, or moccasin and wear it until it is completely dry, resulting in a handsome form-fit. Wet moccasins with rawhide soles need this treatment without fail: you might not be able to get your feet into them if this is not done in a timely way. (Remember when we started talking about getting smoked; the wicked booger analogy applies here.)

It takes extra skill to smoke a finished garment, but some buckskin wearers have been known to re-smoke old, well-worn clothing to restore some of the original color and smell.

The next most distinctive feature of buckskin is that, unlike typical chemical tannage, not only is the hair removed, but the layer that the hair is rooted in—known as "the grain"—is scraped away. As with preparing skins for rawhide, there are wet and dry methods for accomplishing this. The results are similar, but an experienced eye can usually tell the difference: a dry-scraping tool must be very sharp, so it tends to cut deeper and expose the coarser fibers beneath the grain, leaving a somewhat fuzzy surface. A tool for wet scraping is much duller and doesn't cut into the dermal layer, resulting in a finer knap. Quality wet-scrape buckskin will have a lightly-sueded grain-side surface that is springy to the touch. I have been fooling with this material well over 50 years and it still feels like something magic.

With either approach, if this graining phase of the work is not done carefully, it can greatly affect the grade of the product, and it's hard to do anything about it later. It is easy to see the hair, but tricky to see this layer that the hair is growing in, so it's common to find buckskins that are not perfectly scraped. Neither brains nor smoke will effectively penetrate the remaining patches of grain; that resistance often contributes to stiff spots and splotchy color.

It is this hair side of the skin that the great majority of Indian clothing uses on the outside, the same orientation worn by the animal. The texture of this surface, for better or for worse, is a primary factor in appraising the quality of buckskin.

On the flesh side there will always remain a certain amount of the loose, weak tissue we call "membrane". Commercial machinery usually removes this completely, but on hand-fleshed skins this is usually not the case; it adheres more tenaciously on some than on others and often appears like flimsy mats of cotton lint. Its presence can inhibit the penetration of smoke, but because this side is usually not seen on the finished piece, it is considered of little consequence. Unlike grain, superfluous membrane can be handily removed long after the buckskin is made, should that become desirable.

Native people will sometimes make moccasins and clothing using the flesh side out. In this regard, we think especially of several Algonquian tribes—Ojibway and Cree, Cheyenne and Arapaho. Sometimes Kiowa and Comanche. The dermal fibers on the flesh side are very soft and silky, and if the membrane is manicured away, this surface will have a felt-like quality that is very easy to quill and bead.

Regardless of which surface the garment maker decides to put in our or, there is a key fact to always keep in mind when laying out a buckskin clothing project: nature has designed mammals to endure times of feast and famine. This means an animal's skin will expand and contract much more across its belly than down its backbone.

The consequences of this phenomenon are huge when it comes to making garments from soft skins. This is not a situation where one tribe chooses to do something one way and another tribe might decide to do it differently. Studies of Native American clothing show a great intertribal consistency on this point. Skin garments want to have most of their stretch across, not down, the human body, like it worked with the original owner. Whether it is a shoe or the finger of a glove, a legging or a dress, it is critical that the long axis of the body-part be arranged parallel with the head-to-tail axis of the contributing animal. This "line of least stretch" flows down into the legs, which is a consideration if using skin from those areas.

It was in that period 40-50 years ago, when we went from saying Indian-tan to calling it brain-tan, that many tribes lost their last generation of buckskin makers. These were people whose Native tongue was their first language and who had learned this art from their elders before them, from a time when buckskin was a necessary component in their way of life. Prior to the 1970's there were very few contemporary non-Indians who could produce real buckskin.

It is gratifying to know there are still Native people, particularly in the North, who rely on subsistence hunting, who continue to speak their own language and to tan deer, elk, moose and caribou skins in the manner of their ancestors. A few years ago I visited the Shoshone-Bannock trading post at Ft. Hall, Idaho and was pleased to see hundreds of pairs of moccasins, along with other crafts made of Indian-tan, for sale alongside dozens of buckskins in all sizes and smokes. In the back woods of Canada, I am told, one might yet encounter a First Nations hunter wearing smoked moose hide jacket and moccasins. But in a majority of present-day Native communities, the old way of working skins has become increasingly rare, if not lost.

There is presently occurring a brain tanning renaissance led by non-Indians. Dozens of people across this country earn their livelihood by making buckskin and craft items from it. The demand is such that many of them can't keep up with their orders. A good number have learned to make soft, woolly, bison robes using brains and fats, particularly elbow grease. A handful of intrepid individuals have succeeded in re-producing brain-tanned, sinew-sewn, buffalo hide tipis! The skill and commitment that such an effort requires cannot be told with words.

Real buckskin is labor intensive and therefore expensive. We all have relied to some extent on commercial tannage for our projects. Simple economics makes commercial garment leathers very attractive and there is no shame in using them. Given the age-old glamour of the word buckskin, it is no surprise that the modern tanning industry has co-opted the term and advertises its deer and elk hides as such. There has long been a market for commercial products that attempt to give an "Indian-tan look." One of the most satisfactory is a rather recent import known as German-tan, which is made from European red deer, elk and reindeer. This is apparently a combination oil-and-chemical process, with the grain removed by machinery to mimic the surface quality of buckskin; it is much more affordable and accepts a needle almost like the real thing.

It is somewhat ironic that in mid-20th century there arose the hobby of re-enacting the historic culture of the Colonial/Fur trade era, the participants choosing for themselves the moniker of "buckskinners". For the most part, their well-crafted clothing has been made
It is somewhat ironic that in mid-20th century there arose the hobby of re-enacting the historic culture of the Colonial/Fur trade era, the participants choosing for themselves the moniker of "buckskinners". For the most part, their well-crafted clothing has been made
with chrome-tan hides, and only in the last few years have we started to see a transition in their camps to the wearing of actual buckskin. Apparently, Indian hobbyists are increasingly going in this direction as well.

Today it is more reasonable than at any time in recent history for people to make their own buckskin. Some of the best tanners are offering excellent books, videos and tools. As with everything these days, there is a lot of information on the Internet, ranging from pretty good to totally weird. The Braintan.com site is an authentic and responsible source. Reliable educational materials and tools can also be found in the catalogs of mail order trading posts.

One does not need to be a successful hunter to get into this. Small meat packing companies just about everywhere butcher and process deer every fall, and can provide hides and brains. In many areas, classes are offered in buckskin making; some of the best I've seen are being taught by women, the same gender as did most of the tanning in Native societies. It is possible for any determined person with fair strength-of -hand to learn Indian-style tanning. Please consider this if authenticity is important to you.

It's the end of hunting season here now and a lady has just dropped off three green deerskins. Maybe I'll go get a pound of pork brains out of the freezer (any kind will work). I've been sitting at this desk talking about buckskin way too long…. it would be much more fun to go out in the crisp air and do it!

Buck Creek, Nantahala Mountains
December 2013

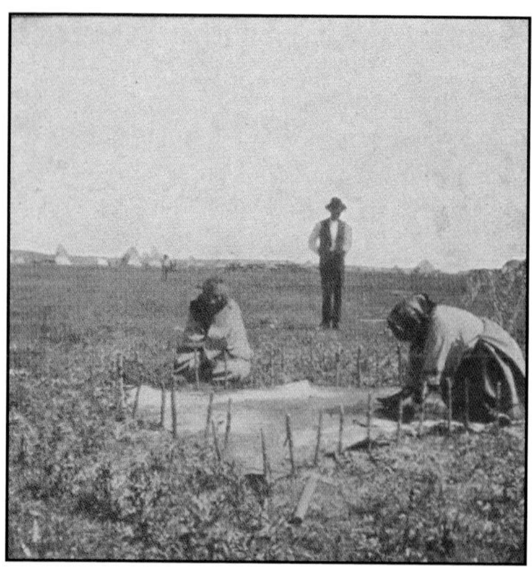

Fleshing a hide

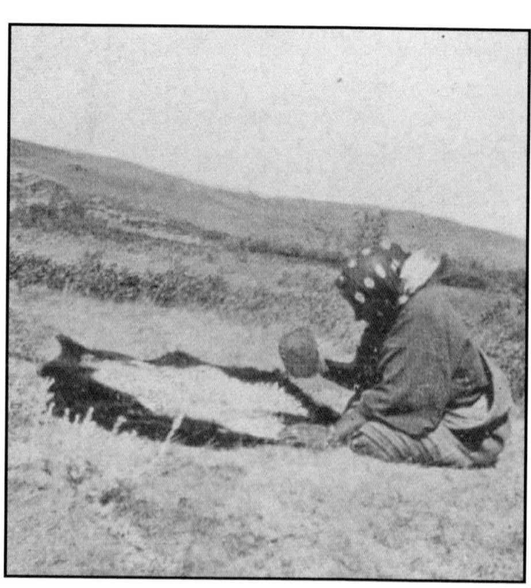

Using a stone scraper

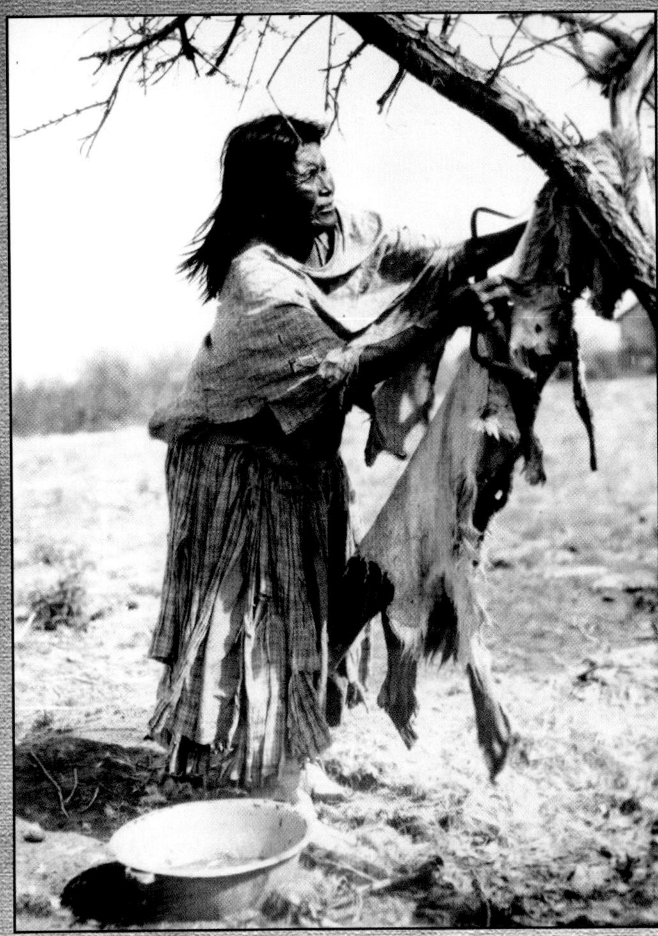

***Wet Scraping** - Interestingly, this woman is scraping with an old draw knife (missing the upper handle), which she is clutching in the middle of the blade with her right hand, while using both hands to adjust the skin on the beam. She is not concerned about cutting herself, because the tool is so dull that is not possible. A wet scrape tools must be of a smooth, hard material but never have a sharp edge, so they were commonly made out of modified rib & leg bones & even very hard woods. Her moccasins are obscured in the photo, but are probably much like those in Figure 7 on page 64. Courtesy of Arizona State Museum University of Arizona, Negative No. 64461.*

***Dry Scraping** - Jeanette Little Crow is bent over in classic Plains posture for dry scraping, removing the hair and grain with over-lapping strokes of her tool. The tool handle is made from an elk antler, with the head shaped into a strong crook at the point where a tine branched off. For over 150 years, her people have used steel blades for this purpose, though the form of this tool is much older. Whether the blade is made of steel or stone or obsidian, it requires frequent maintenance; the cutter must be resharpened often and if it becomes slightly loose, the buckskin lashing is retied. To understand how her moccasins are made, see pages 70 - 71. Courtesy of State Historical Society of North Dakota (00039-0056).*

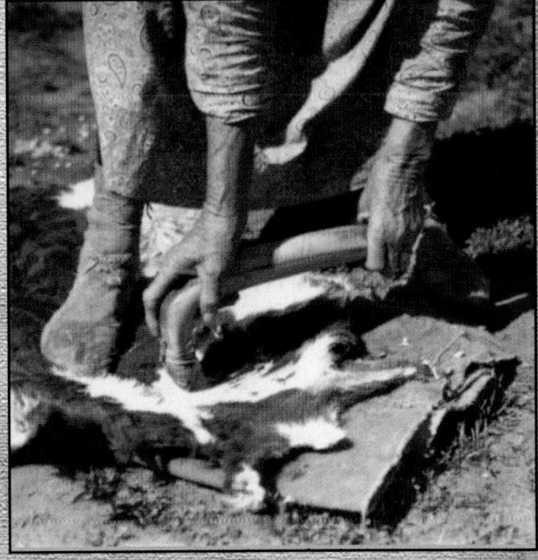

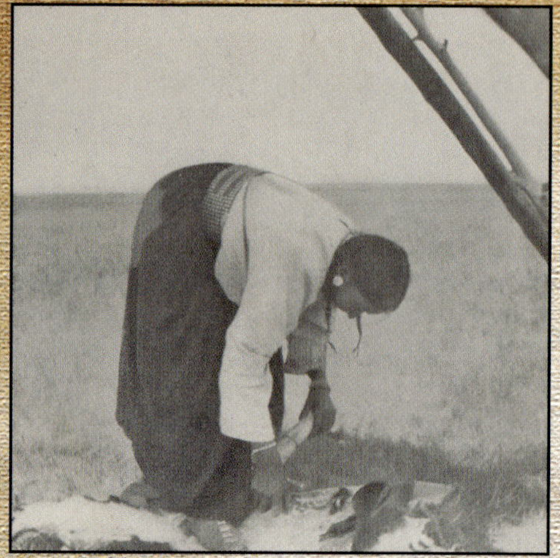

Scraping the hide

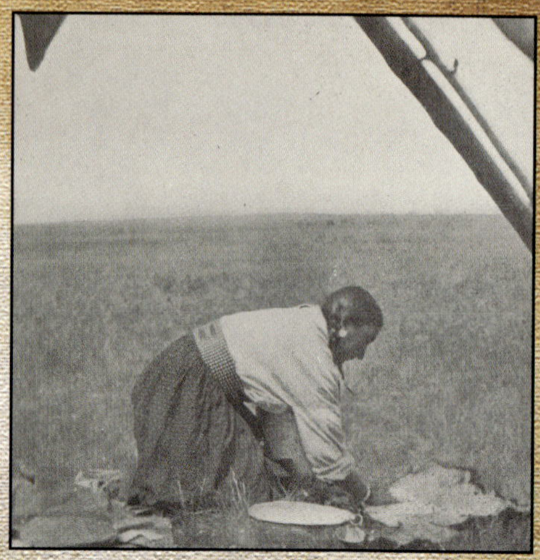

Applying the fat

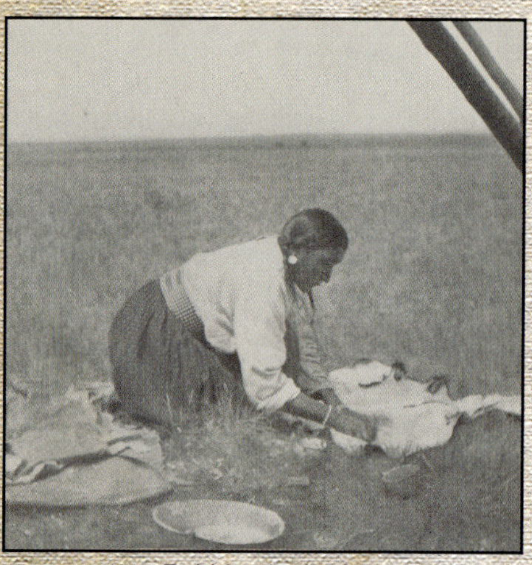

Rubbing in the fat

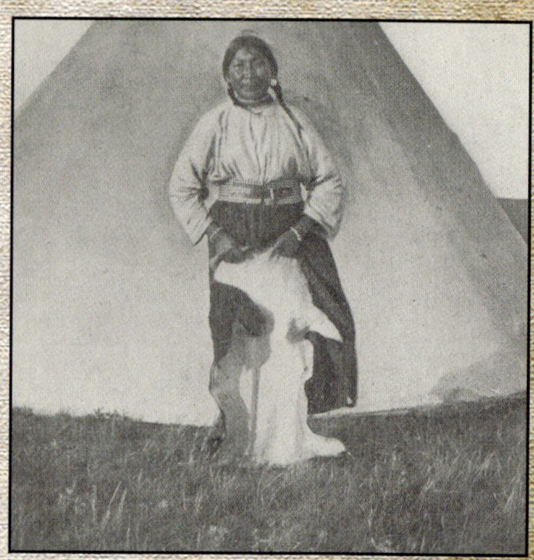

Stretching the hide

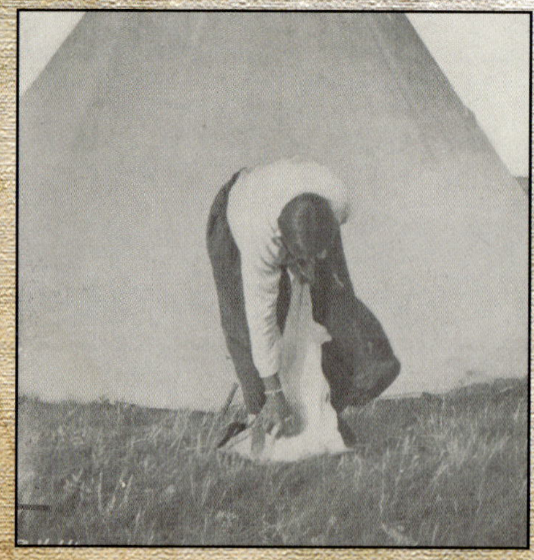

Graining the surface

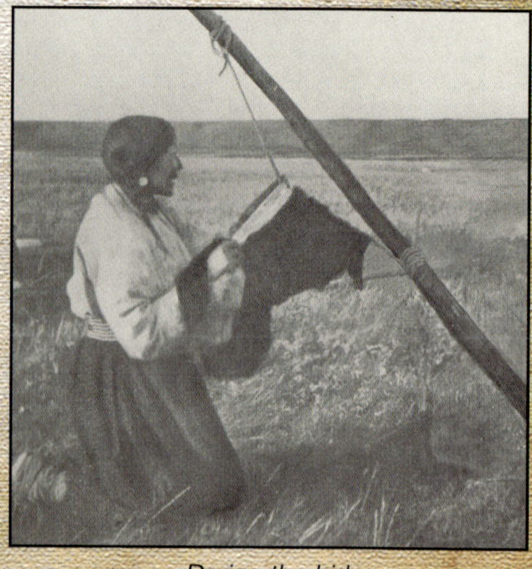

Drying the hide

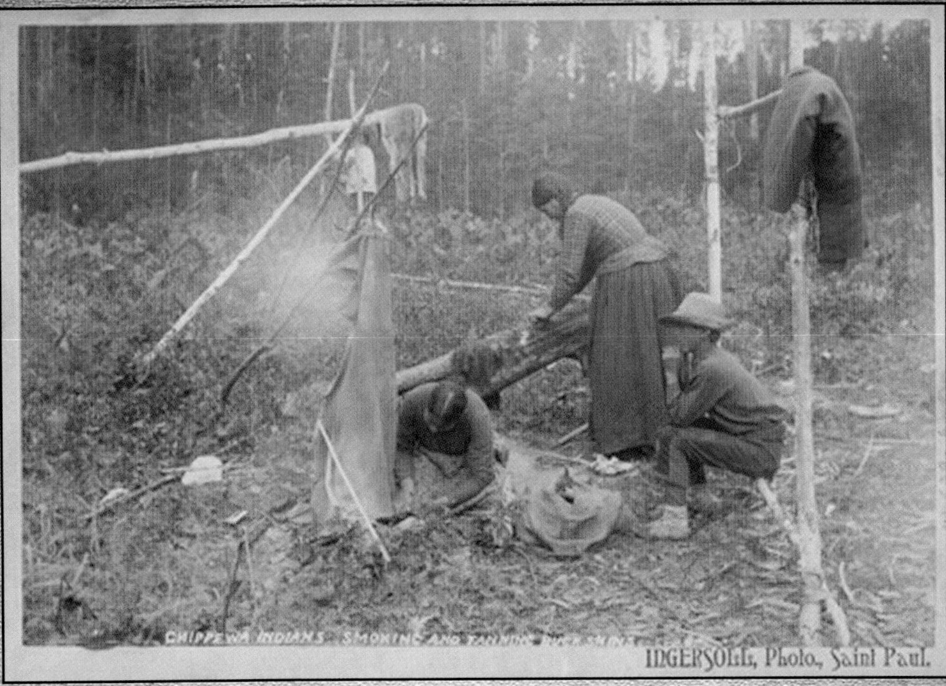

INGERSOLL, Photo., Saint Paul.

Chippewa Indians tanning and smokng hides.

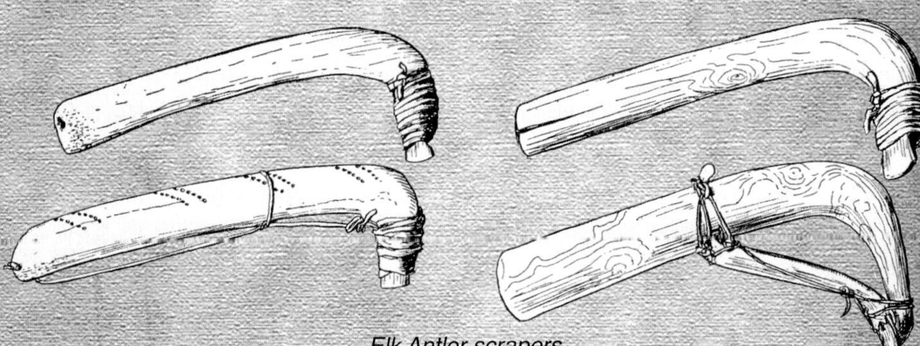

Elk Antler scrapers

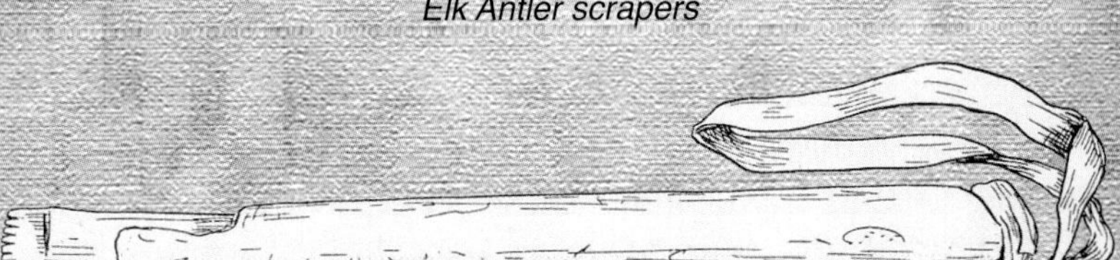

Hide covered iron scraper

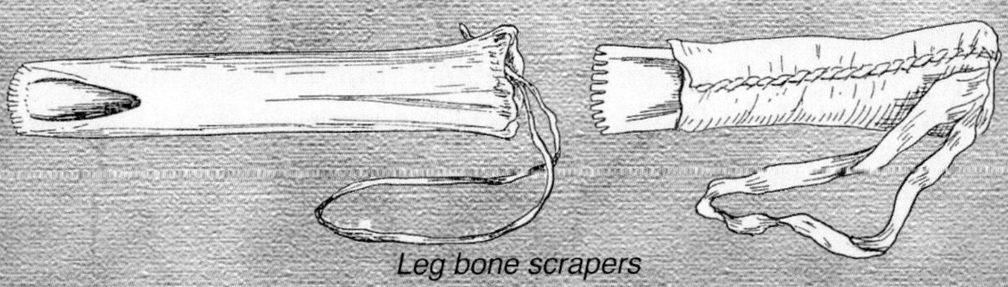

Leg bone scrapers

Early Moccasin Types

Promontory Moccasin

This 900 year old Slipper-type moccasin was discovered in Promontory Cave, Utah. Dating from 1225 - 1275 AD, it is constructed of bison hide with the hair turned inside. This example features an added upper flap which is not shown in the illustrations.
Natural History Museum of Utah

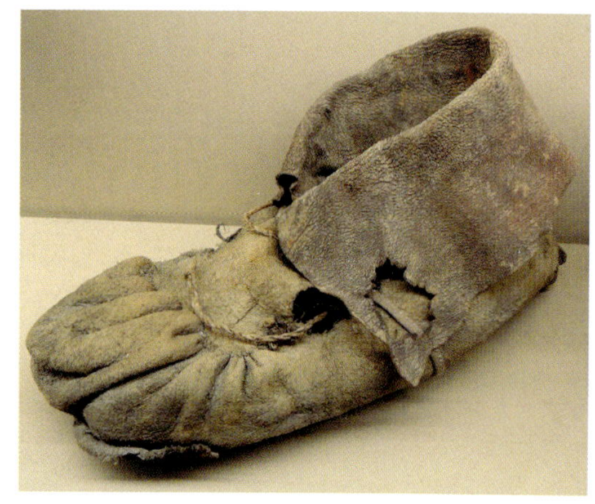

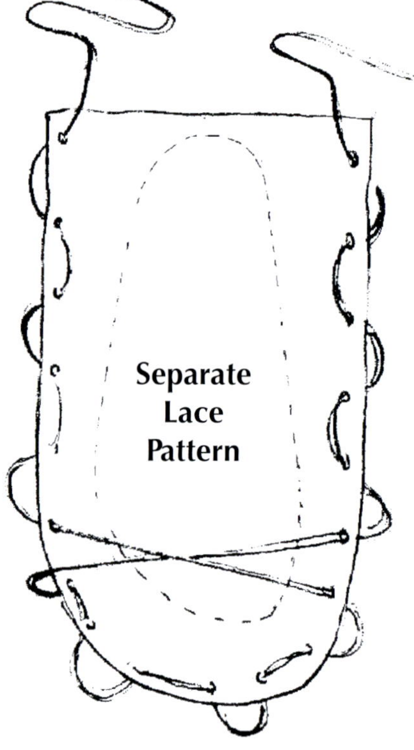

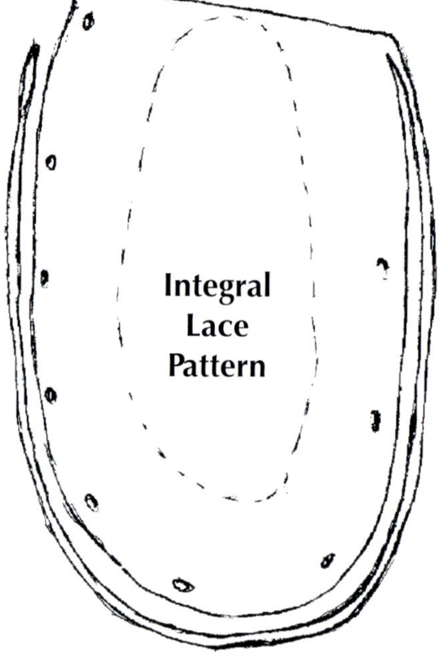

Finishing separate lace moccasin

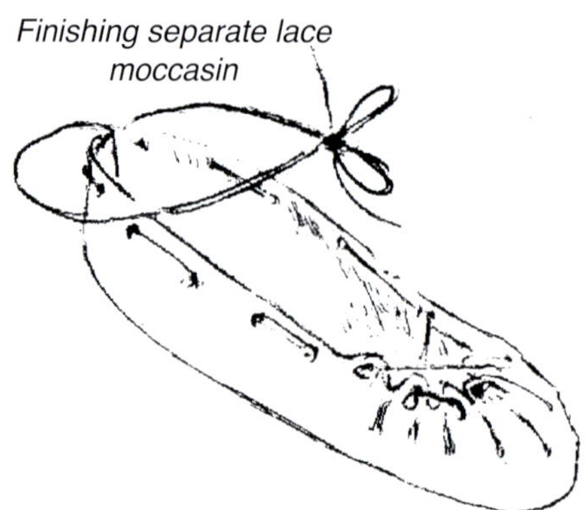

Finishing integral lace moccasin

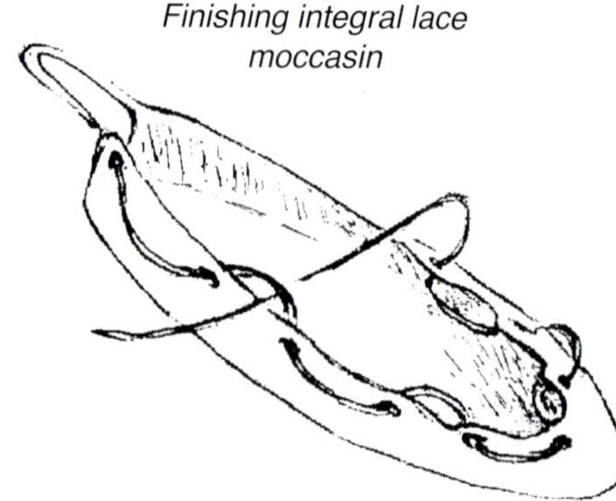

Simple "PUCKER" Slipper Type

1. Trace foot on paper. See general instructions.
2. **A' B'** is 1/2" to 1" less than **A B**. See Fig. G-2, Page 13.
3. **L M** is foot length (tracing) plus 1/2" at heel, plus 2" to 2 1/2" at toe, or measure from heel over big toe to joint of big toe (base). See Fig. G-3, page 13.
4. Connect **A' M** and **B' M** with a gentle curve.
5. Fold pattern on line **L M** as this can be symmetrical. There is no left or right.
6. Trace two patterns on leather (See leather instructions on page 14.)
7. With an awl make holes about 1/4 to 3/8 inches apart and use a heavy strong thread; lace in and out. (See **Fig. 1**.)
8. Draw up thread, as in **Fig. 2**, as tightly as possible. Tie the two ends of thread with a good knot.
9. Sew heel by joining **X X'** and sew down to **L**. (This produces a pointed heel.) Tie off thread.
10. Make second moccasin in same manner.

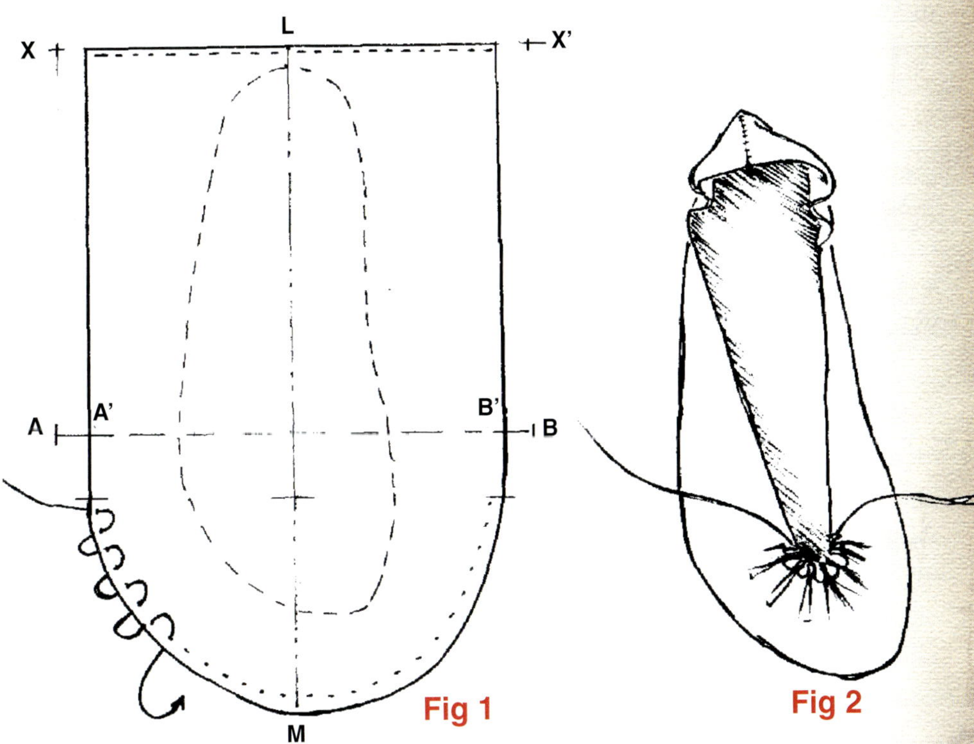

Fig 1

Fig 2

Moccasins from Hogup Cave, Utah

(Dew Claw Type)

Twenty-three moccasins were recovered from Hogup Cave and classified into three categories: Hock moccasins, Fremont moccasins, and Hogup moccasins. The Hogup type, illustrated here, were made from a single piece of hide from the lower leg of a deer, tanned with the dew claws on. that is folded over the foot and sewn together across the toe. A separate outer sole was added to the basic piece and an ankle wrap was sewn around the upper part of the basic piece to give the moccasin a bootlike appearance.

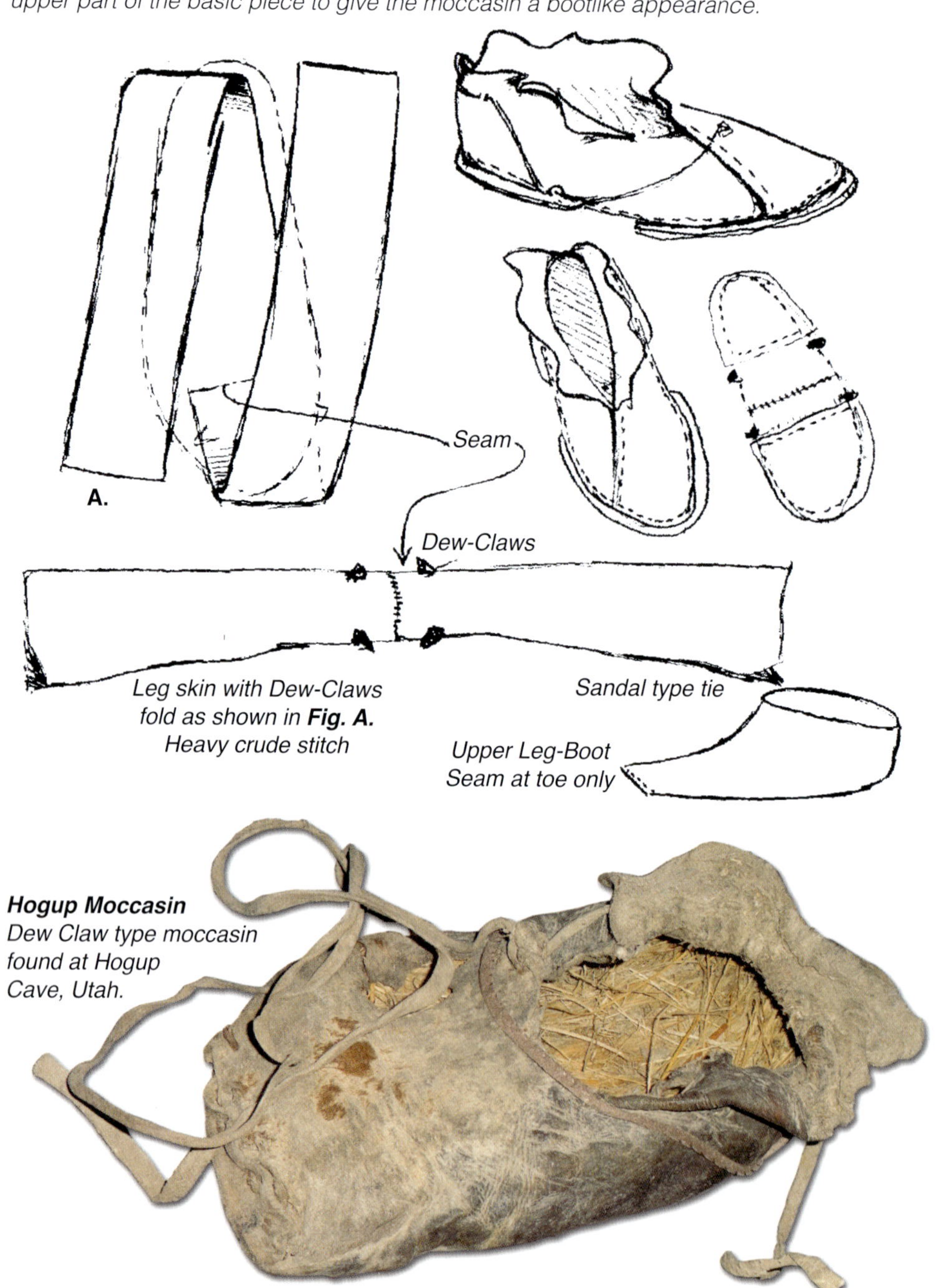

Hogup Moccasin
Dew Claw type moccasin found at Hogup Cave, Utah.

GENERAL INSTRUCTIONS
for Making Moccasins

The following instructions should be used for laying out and making all of the moccasin designs in this book. Special instruction will be found with each pattern, and heel and tongue detail sheets illustrate particular methods of handling these areas. Illustrations on page 18 show stitches commonly found on old moccasins. It is recommended that the novice use the simple "whip stitch" before attempting the more complicated stitches.

The following steps should be observed for laying out all moccasins, unless a precut kit is used or you are making the plains moccasons begening on pages 33 and 58.

1. Place a large piece of paper on the floor.
2. Place either foot on the paper, (See drawing **G-1**)
3. Hold pencil perpendicular and trace foot outline.
4. Draw in line **L M** as shown in **Fig. G-2**.
5. (For a foot that is longer than 9 inches, add 3/4" to heel and 1/2" to the toe.
6. Mark these measurements on paper on line **L M**. (These may vary with design.)
7. Draw line **A B** as shown in **Fig. G-2** and **G-3**. Use string and measure circumference of foot at the thickest point, where you would tie a shoe string.
8. Mark this measurement on line **A B**. Double the string and place loop end on the center line **L M**. The other end should give location of **A** or **B**.
9. **L M** and **A B** are needed for all moccasins to produce a good fit.
10. Turn to the moccasin design to be copied and make your pattern of the foot tracing. Note the special instructions.
11. If heavy leather is used add 1/4" to pattern along **A B** measurements to allow for seams.
12. After laying out the pattern on paper and rechecking measurements cut out the pattern. Do not cut out any tongue drawn on pattern in dotted line.
13. It is highly recommended that hides be stretched before cutting. This will help prevent your moccasins from stretching with wear and becoming baggy and too wide or too long. Lay leather out on a large surface such as a table top. Place the paper pattern on the leather as shown in **G-4**. (Position pattern lengthwise along the back line, never on a bias or at right angles to the hide.)
14. When the design calls for a left and right pattern, use the same pattern but be certain to turn the pattern over before tracing the second pattern on the leather.
15. Lay pattern against the edges of the leather- to save leather- and trace the second piece as close as possible for the same reason. Make sure to use the part of the hide that is an even weight and not too thin for both uppers and soles.
16. Be sure to check leather under pattern for cuts, thin spots, or holes before tracing the pattern. (Ballpoint pen marks cannot be removed except by cutting off.)
17. Trace all patterns as close together as possible and cut out.
18. Special instructions should be noted at this point.
19. Sewing is started at the toe after centering at point **M** and going to the heel. This allows the novice to make adjustments at the heel. Be sure to tie off at the end of each thread when beginning.
20. Special sewing instructions are found with each drawing.
21. All soft soled or woodland type moccasins are made snug as they loosen with wearing. The hard sole and the shaped sole moccasin are made a bit larger because the sole piece will have less give and stretch than the soft sole type.

22. Tie Strings - See **Fig. G-11** on page 23. Tie strings are cut from scrap leather 4" or 5" in diameter. DO NOT USE flank leather as it is weak and stretches. Cut string about 3/8" wide and about 36" long. Test by stretching before using. Note special instructions for attaching tie strings for each design. See Tongue Detail sheet on page 25.

23. Holes for tie strings are never cut. Always make holes with an awl or a pointed tool.

Figures G-5 to **G-8** on page 22 illustrate the relationship between sole and vamp-upper piece or sole and insert.
Figure G-6 shows both sole and vamp being the same width, and together the two pieces equal the circumference of the foot at line **A B**.
Figure G-6A shows the vamp and a shaped sole in the style of the Apache, Navajo and Pueblo. Together these two pieces equal the circumference.
Figure G-7 shows sole the same width as foot tracing and the vamp must be wider to complete the circumference.
Figure G-8 shows sole (e.g. Yukon Type) much wider than foot outline and the insert completes the circumference. With all these measurements 1/4" should be added to allow for seams which take away from circumference measurements.

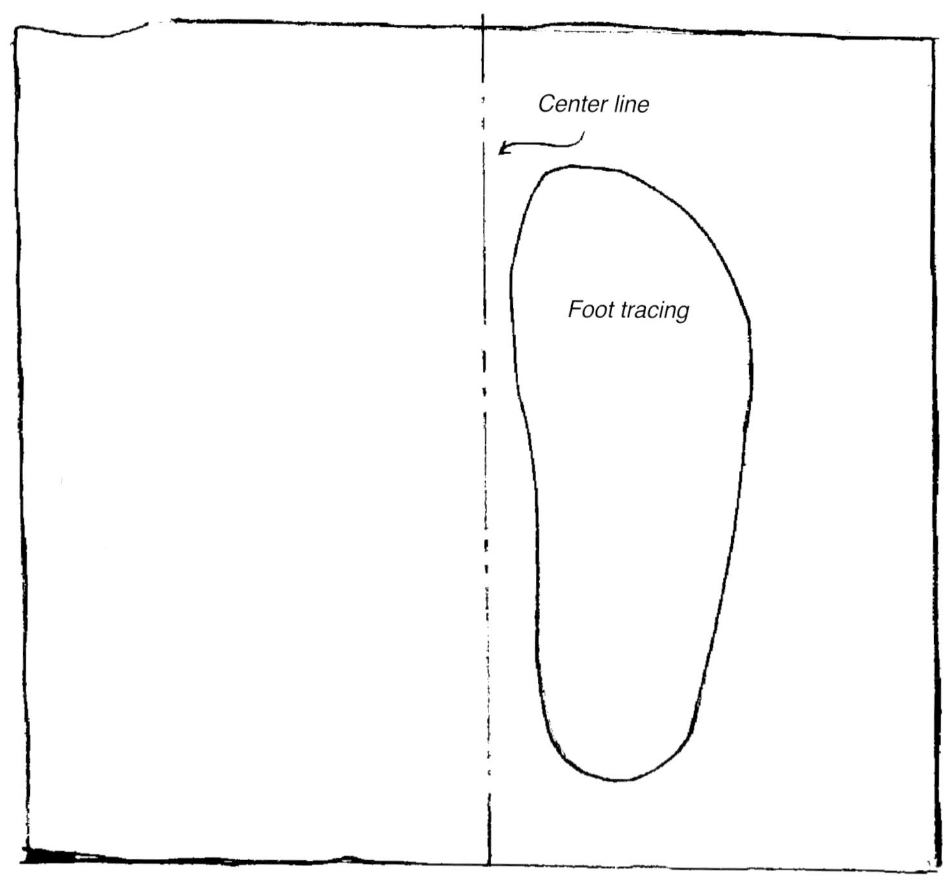

G-1

GENERAL INFORMATION

For all Leather Footwear

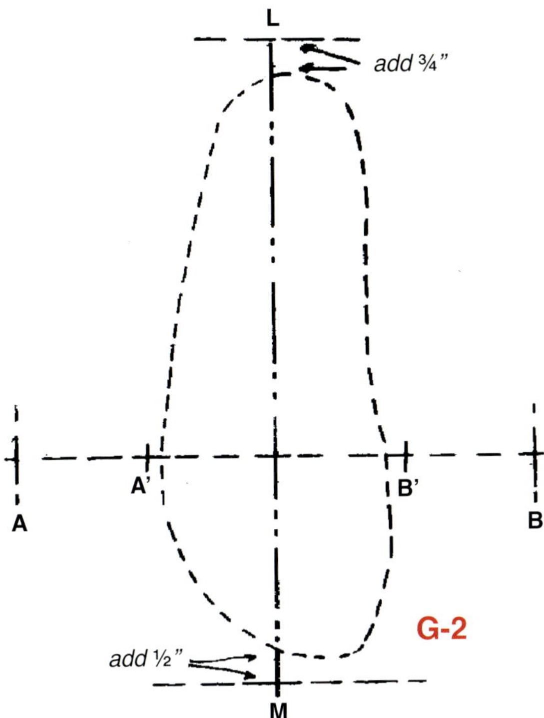

A B = Largest circumference of the foot at this point. This measurement must be considered in all designs to obtain the proper fit.
A' B' will vary with pattern, but is always less than **A B**.
L M = Length measurement of leather. This measurement will vary slightly with different designs.

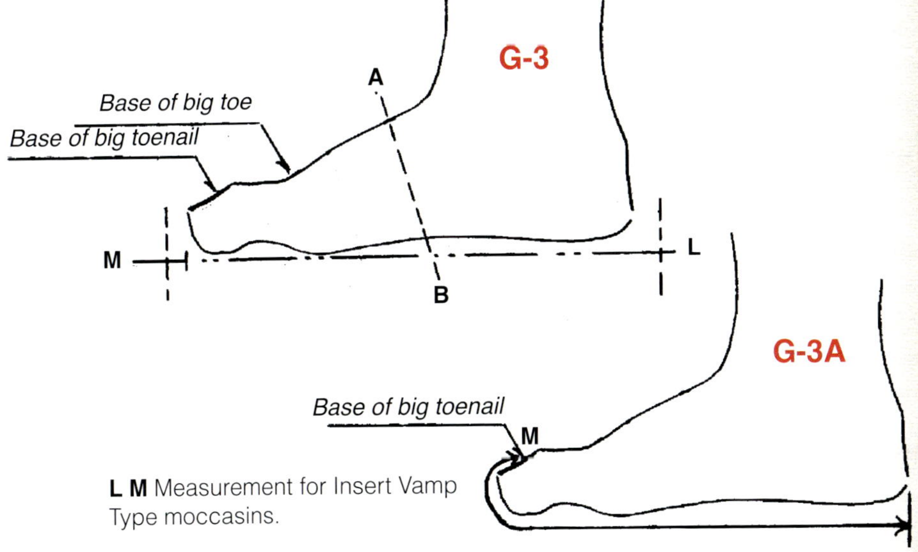

L M Measurement for Insert Vamp Type moccasins.

Leather Layout Instructions

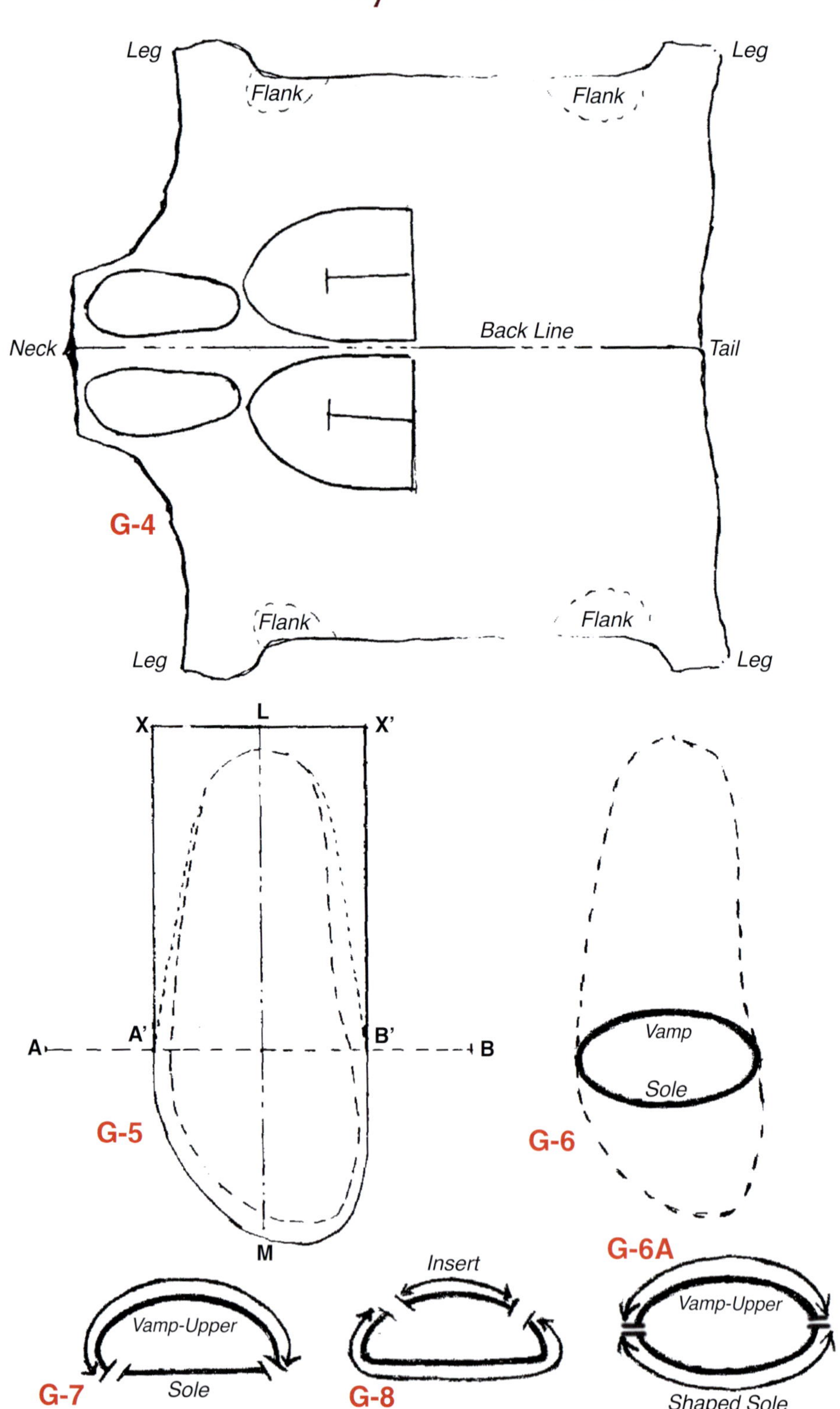

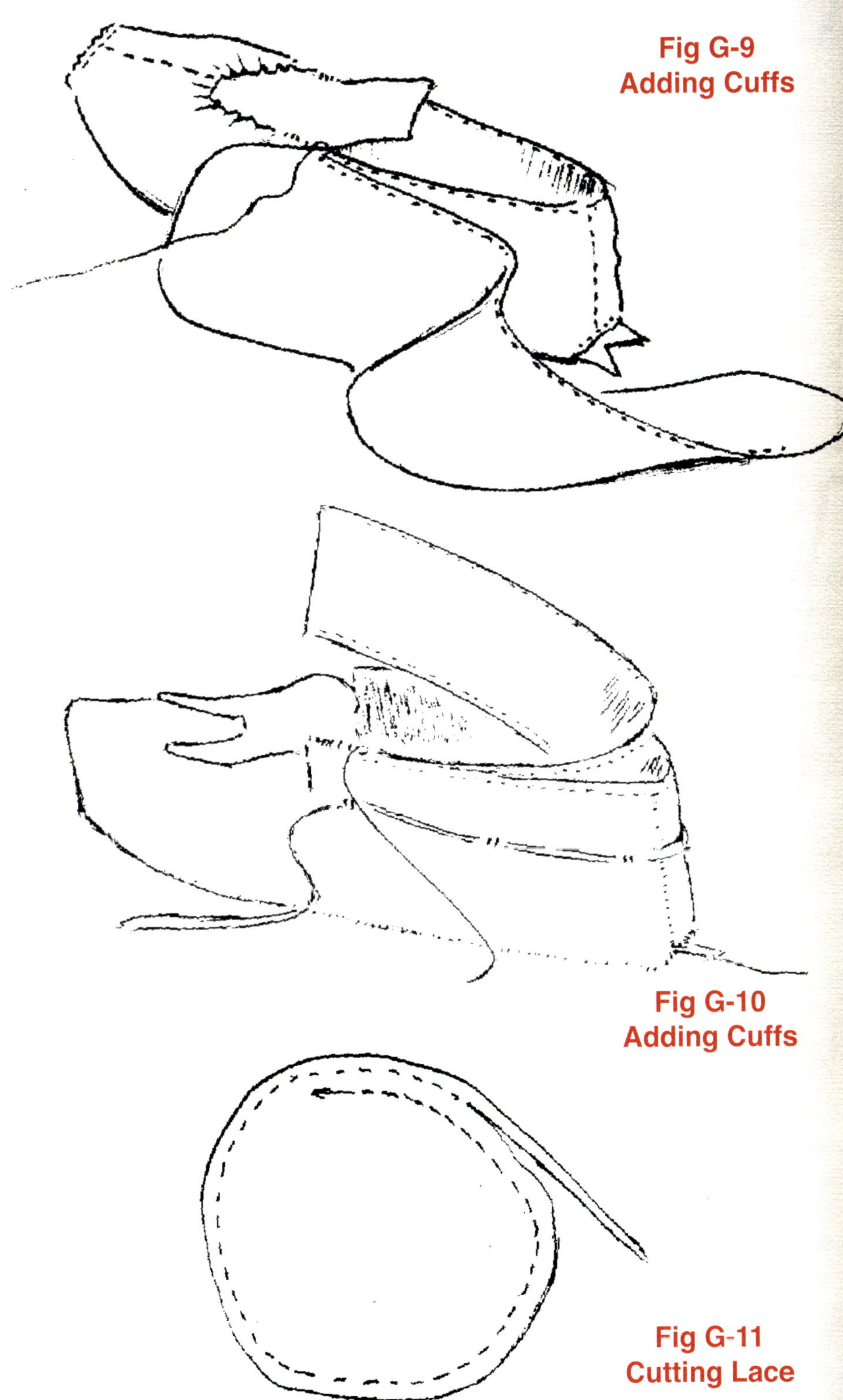

Fig G-9
Adding Cuffs

Fig G-10
Adding Cuffs

Fig G-11
Cutting Lace

Heel Details

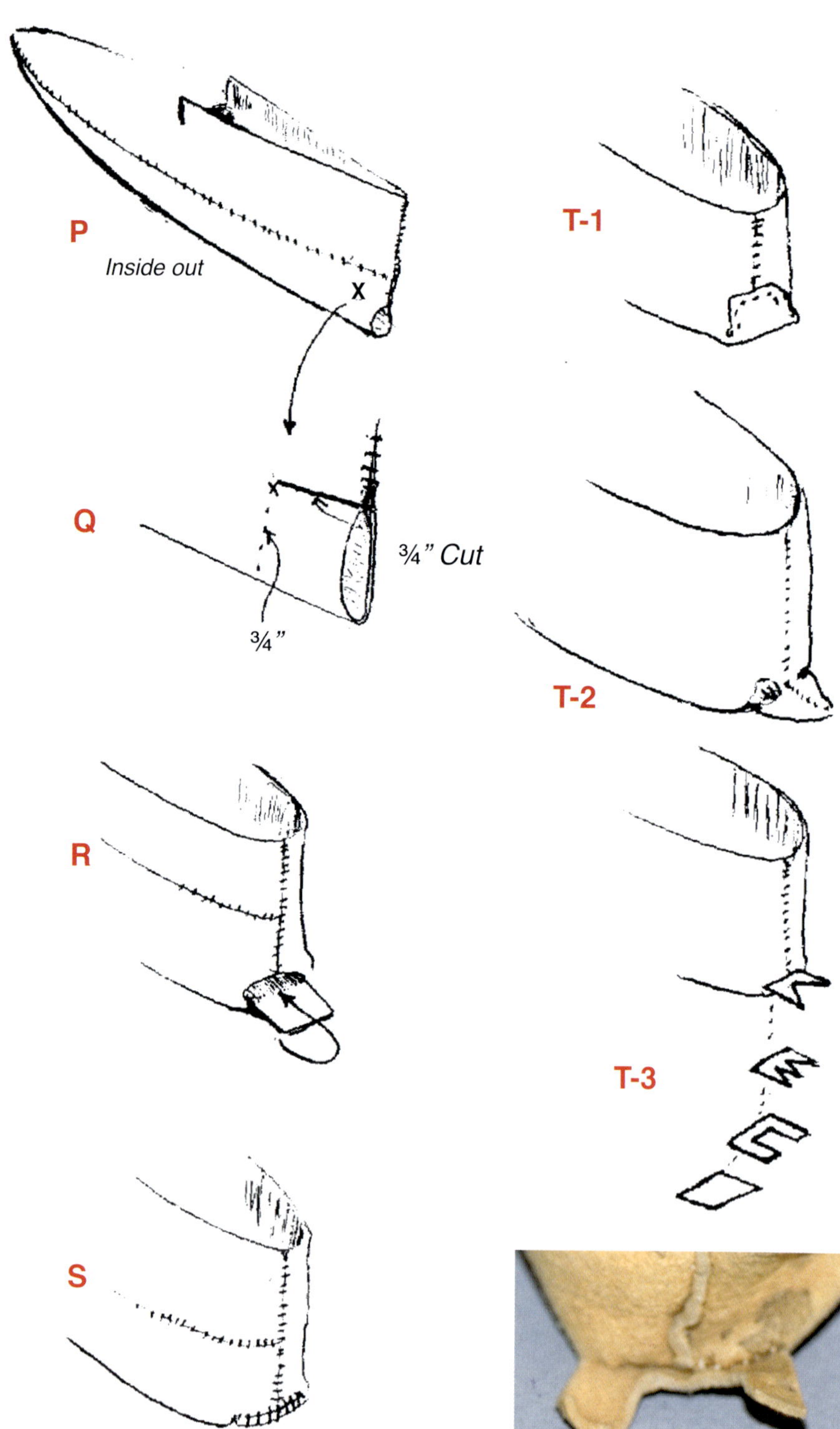

Tongue and Tie-String Details

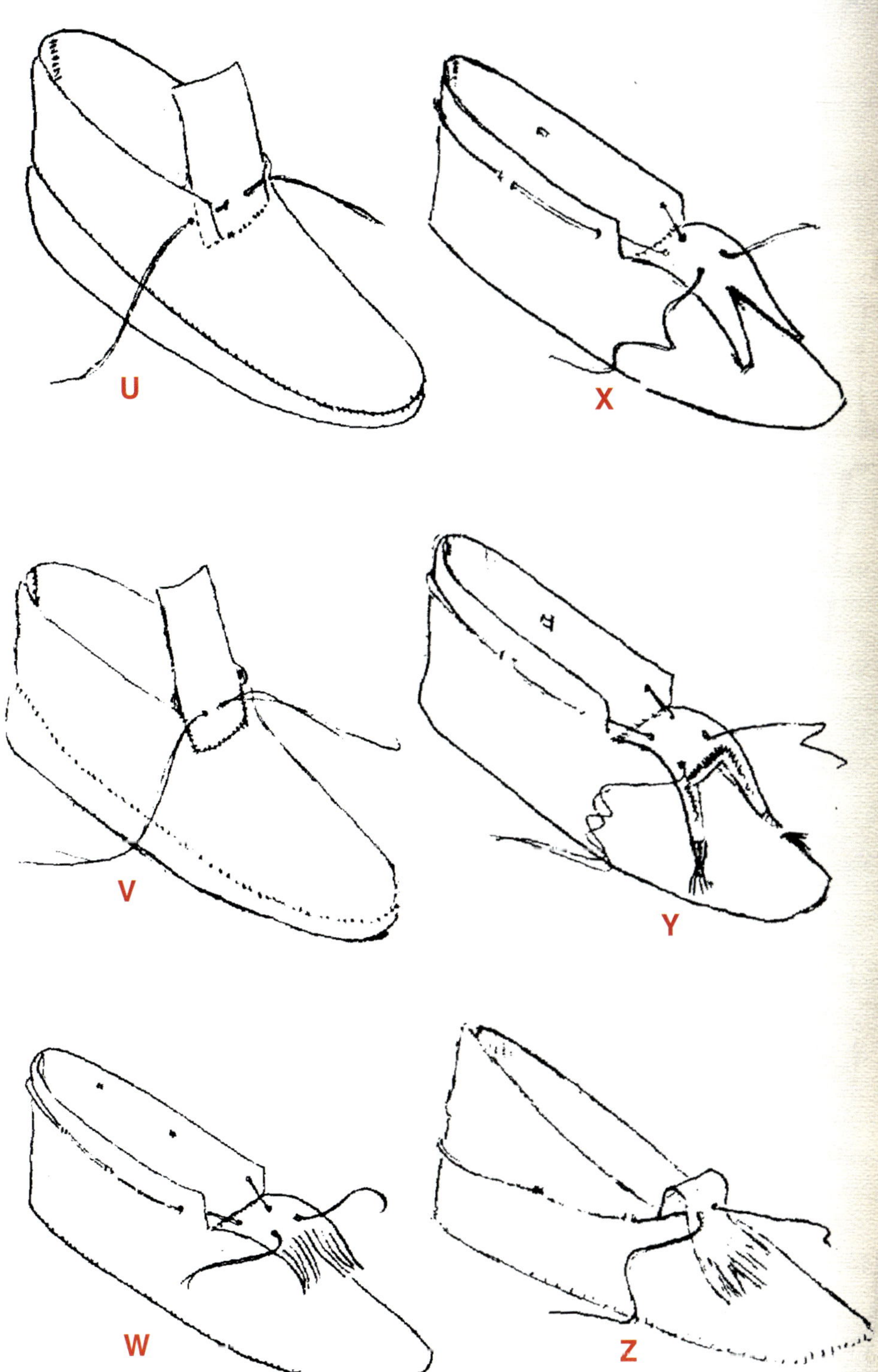

Stitches Commonly Used for Moccasins

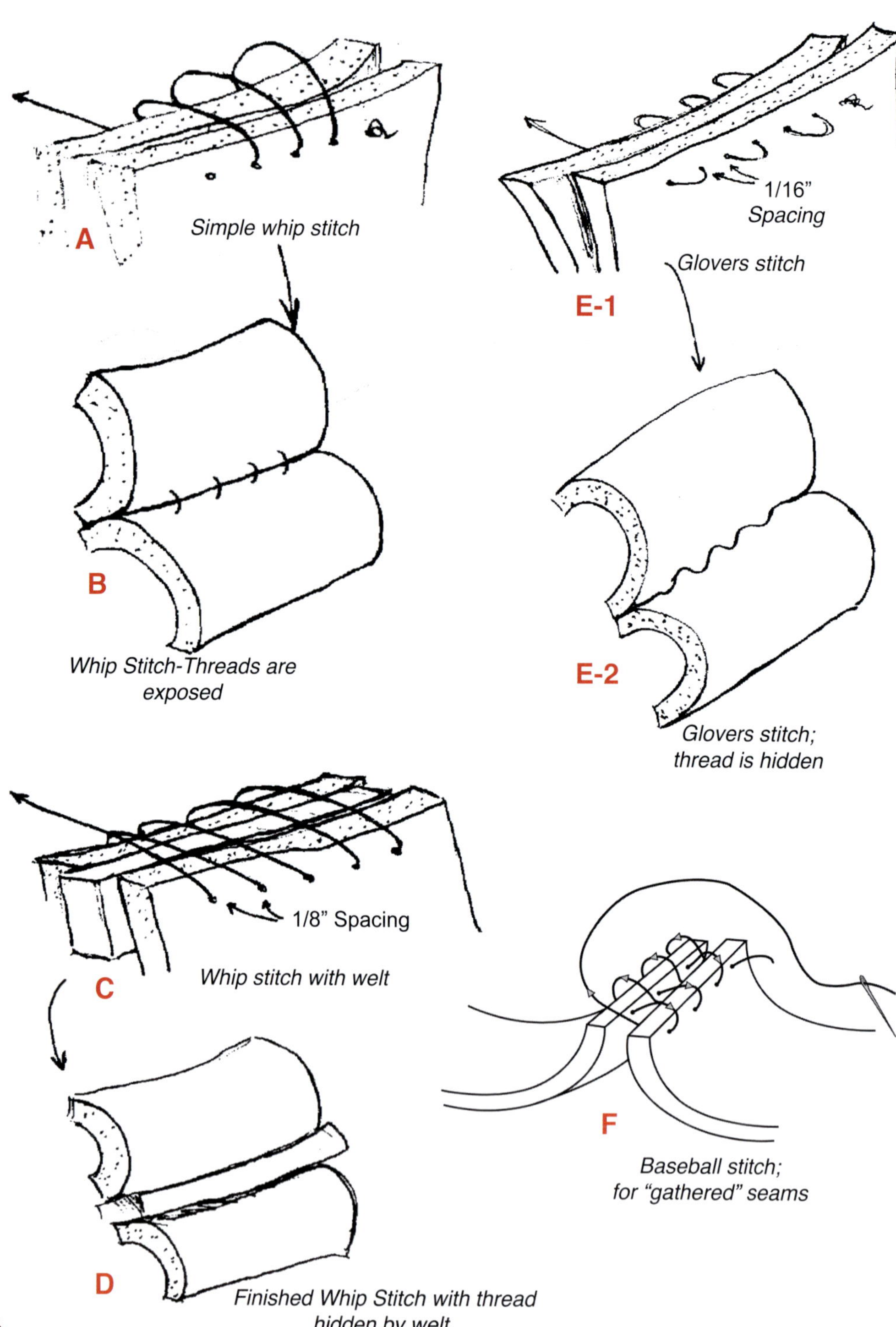

Sewing Parfleche (Rawhide) Soles

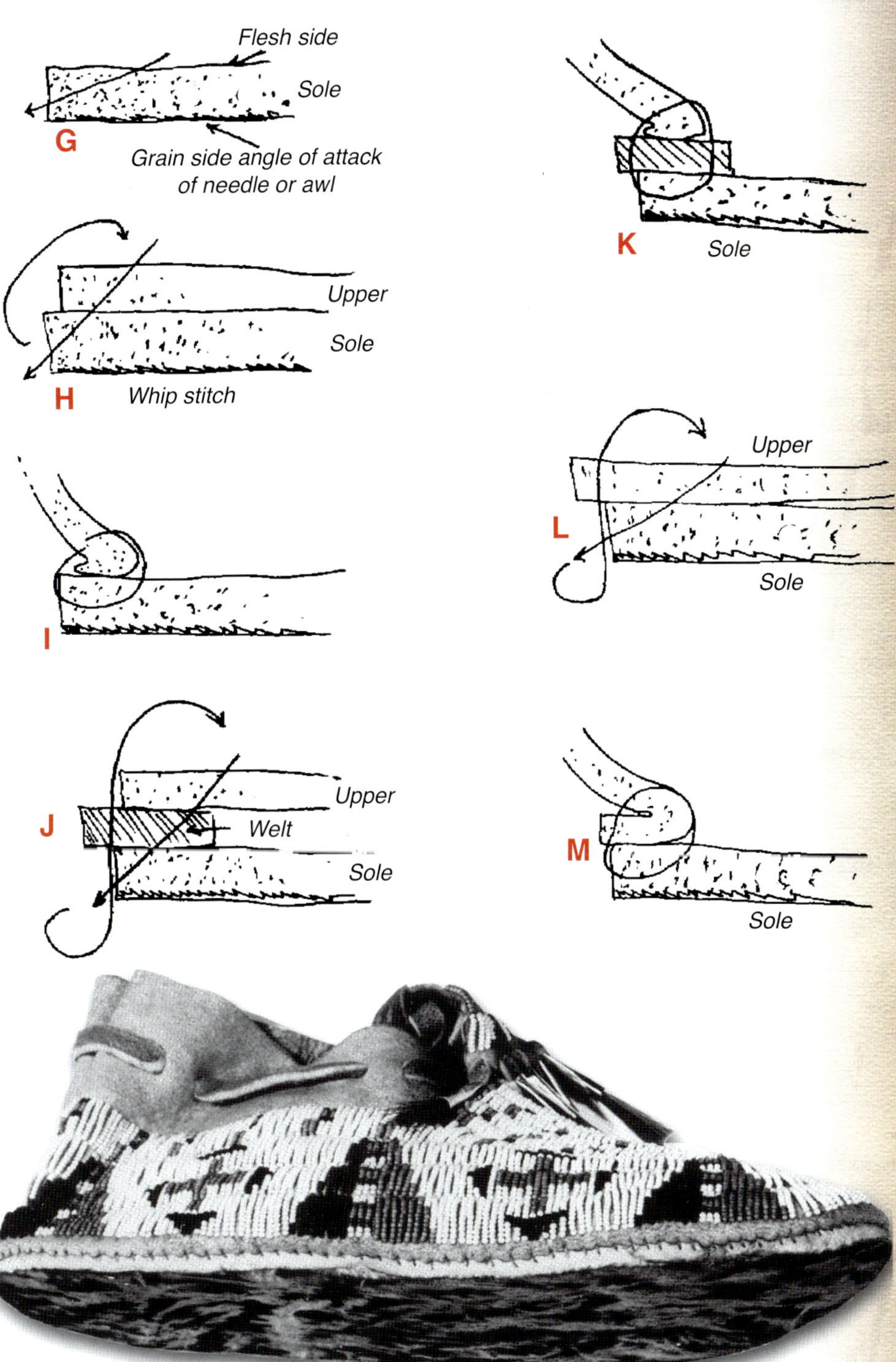

*This view of a completed hard-sole moccasin without a welt illustrates the type of stitching shown in illustrations **"H"** and **"I"**, above.*

Eastern Woodlands

Simple Center Seam

Pointed Toe

This style moccasin, dating as early as the 18th century, was common to many different tribes of the Eastern Woodlands, Great Lakes and Prairie regions of the U.S., including the Iroquois Confederacy (Mohawk, Oneida, Onondaga, Cayuga and Seneca), Miami, Delaware, Potawatomi, Otoe, Iowa, Sac & Fox, Shawnee, Huron and Kickapoo. Early Huron, Delaware and Shawnee styles are typically of the "stand-up cuff" types, which dated from the 18th century and continued in use into the 19th century. Other types began to appear as early as 1830 among the Great Lakes and Missouri River Tribes, evolving into the "side flaps" style as illustrated in the accompanying photos, with both types being in use simultaneously at this early date. Everyday moccasins were rather plain, without the heavily decorated side flaps of formal dress types shown in some of the accompanying photographs. These plain flaps were often turned up, wrapped and tied for additional protection.

1. See General Instructions on page 20.
2. **A B** is full circumference.
3. **L M** is (for average 9 to 12 inch foot size) length of foot plus 1/4".
4. Note there is no heel cut.
5. Sewing: Fold on line **L M**, inside out.
6. Sew from **M** to **A B** to about one inch from flaps; tie off thread securely.
7. Sew heel from **X X'** to **L**.
8. Turn moccasin right side out.
9. Sew second moccasin in same manner.
10. Note the 3 foot outlines in **Fig. 1**. The left and right tracings are more important positions as they will show the amount of leather needed to cover the foot.
11. **Fig. 2** shows the completed moccasin.

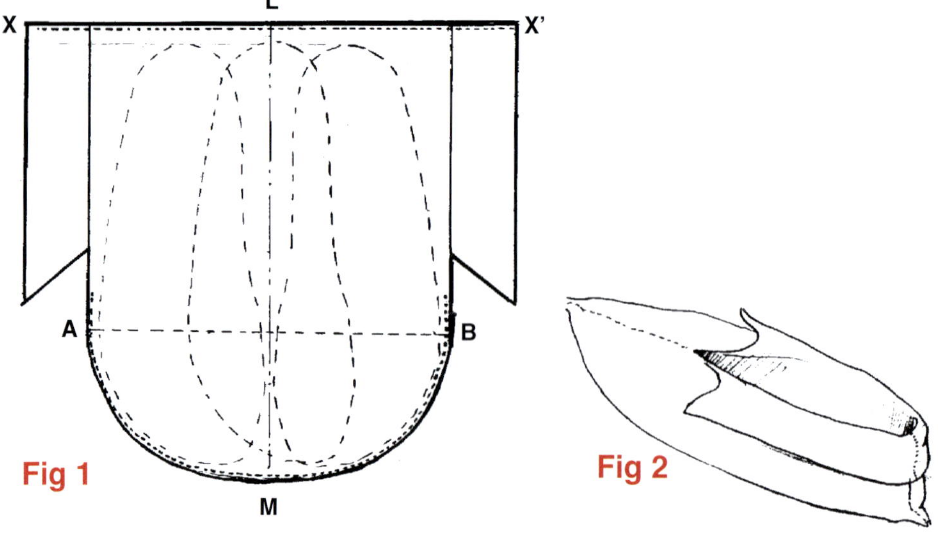

Fig 1

Fig 2

Oneida - Iroquoian

Center Seam

Part of the Six Nation Confederacy, the Oneida, "People of the Standing Stone", are one of the founding nations of the Iroquois Confederacy in the area of upstate New York. Under federal and state pressure, many Oneida resettled in Wisconsin in the early 1800s while others who had allied with the British had already migrated to Canada. In the 21st century, the Oneida have four independent tribal groups in New York and Wisconsin, as well as Ontario, Canada. Some of the Oneidas now live on their reservation south of Oneida in Madison County, New York with other members living on the Onondaga Nation Reservation, south of Syracuse.

1. See General Instructions.
2. **A B** is full circumference.
3. **L M** is about 1-1/4" longer than foot tracing, (This is for a foot length of 9" to 12") Side flaps can vary from 1 to 3 inches in width.
4. Notice that the layout is similar to that of a "side seam". The leather requirement is exactly the same as the side seam; only the sewing varies.
5. Cut two identical pieces of leather from the same pattern.
6. Fold leather inside out on **L M** ; sew from **M** to **A B**.
7. Leave foot opening large {more than 1/2 the length of moccasin)
8. Sew **X X'** to **L**.
9. See Heel Detail on page 24 for sewing heel.
10. Turn moccasin right side out and cut the heel as shown in **Fig. 2**.

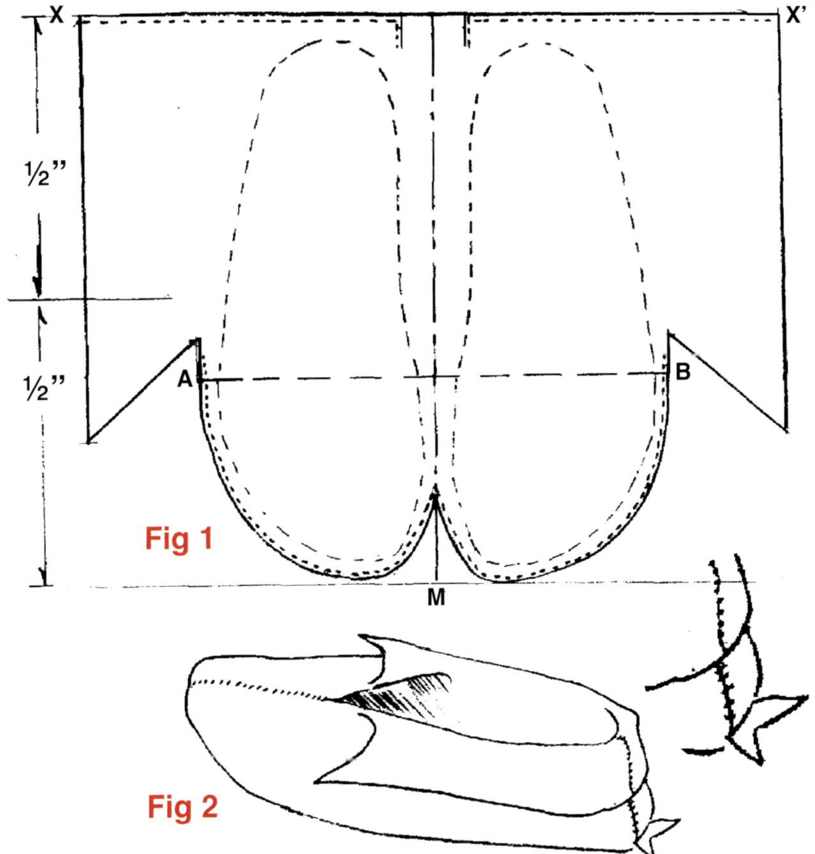

Iroquois

Center Seam

The Iroquois Confederacy, also known as the Six Nations, was a historically powerful group who formed a league of six distinct nations: the Mohawk, Oneida, Onondaga, Cayuga, Seneca and Tuscarora. Originally "Five Nations", they are believed to have emerged as distinct tribes by the 15th century or earlier, with each having a distinct territory and function within the League. Iroquois influence originally extended into Canada, westward into the Great Lakes and down both sides of the Allegheny Mountains into Virginia and Kentucky. The League still exists today, with the people living in different areas of New York, Wisconsin, Northeastern Oklahoma and Ontario, Canada.

1. Trace outline of foot.
2. Measure **A B** (see General Instructions on pages 19 - 21)
3. Measure **L M** (allow 3/4" at heel and about 1-1/2" beyond the big toe, or, allow enough material to cover the heel and lap the big toe completely.
4. Place these measurements on foot tracing.
5. **C X** measure is found by adding 3/4" at heel and 1/2" at toe of foot tracing.
6. Point **A** is 1/2 the distance of **C X** .
7. Line **A B** is circumference of foot.
8. **A'B'** plus tongue-insert piece is equal to **A B**.
9. Angle between **H K** and **H'K'** is between 100 - 120 degrees. See **Fig. 1**.
10. The arc between **K** and **K'** is about 1/2 the distance between **A'** and **B'**.
11. Fold the paper on line **L M** and cut pattern so both sides will be symmetrical.
12. Do not cut out the tongue pattern. See Step 22.
13. Make 2 tracings of pattern on leather and cut. (CAUTION: See General Instructions for placing pattern on leather, page 19, **Step 13** and page 22, **G-4**.
14. There is no left or right foot to this design.
15. Sew by folding leather inside out. Bring **H** and **H'** together. See **Fig. 8**.
16. Use 1/8" whip stitch on all seams, except where gathering is necessary.
17. Sew **H H'** to **K K'**. **Fig. 3**.
18. Turn moccasin right side out. Bring center of toe flap to point **K K'**.
19. Close toe with a gathering stitch: 1/8" stitch on short run and 1/4" stitch on long run (**M**). See **Fig. 3**. Tie off each end of thread.
20. Sew heel next. Turn moccasin inside out. Bring **X X'** together. Sew down to heel cut using 1/8" whip stitch. Turn moccasin right side out.
21. Cut the tongue/insert out next. Make the tongue pattern as shown in **Fig. 1**. Determine tongue width so that **A' B'** plus tongue equal **A B** (circumference).
22. Sew tongue to moccasin at point **A'** where the tongue piece begins to taper. Use gathering stitch: 1/4" stitch on moccasin piece and 1/8" stitch on tongue.
23. The foot opening should be 1/2 the length of the moccasin.
24. Turn heel tab up and catch with a few stitches.
25. Top extensions are added. (See **Fig. G-9**, page 23)

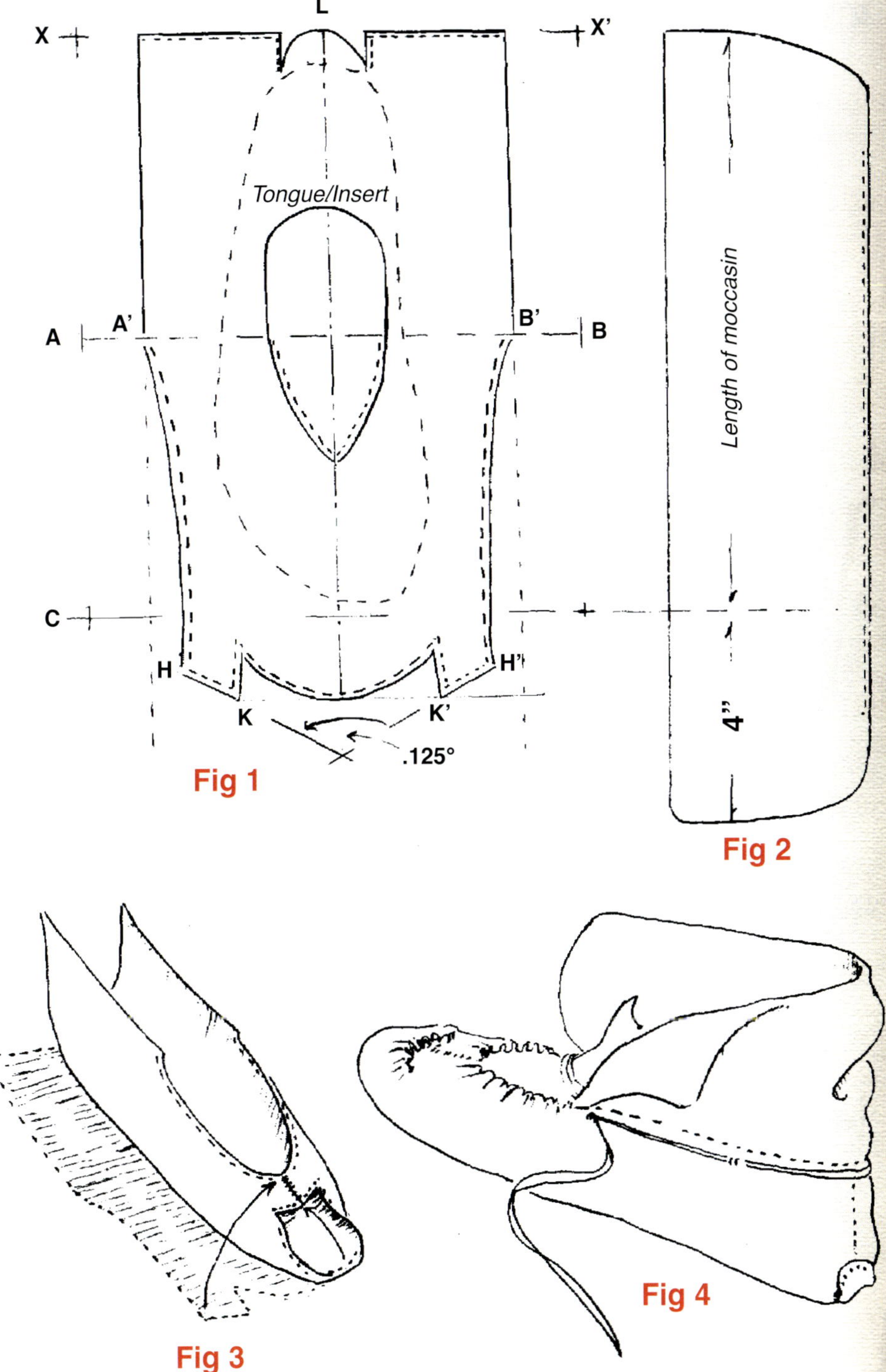

Fig 1

Fig 2

Fig 3

Fig 4

Iroquoian

Small Insert Vamps - Pointed Heel

1. See General Instructions.
2. A B = circumference of foot.
3. A'B' + insert = **A B (Fig. 1 and 2)**
4. L M is length of leather from heel and around and up to base of big toe nail. See **Fig. G-3A**, page 21.
5. Sew inside out if the leather is light weight. Sew outside out if leather is heavy.
6. Place insert **M** on sole **M**. Use 1/8" stitch on insert piece and use 1/4" stitch on sole piece.
7. Sew from **M** to point beyond **A** or **B**.
8. The foot opening remaining should be 1/2 the length of finished moccasin.
9. If the moccasin is inside out, bring **X** and **X'** together and sew from **X X'** to **L**.
10. Turn moccasin right side out.
11. This heel is pointed as shown in **Fig. 3**.
12. Cuffs may be added if desired.

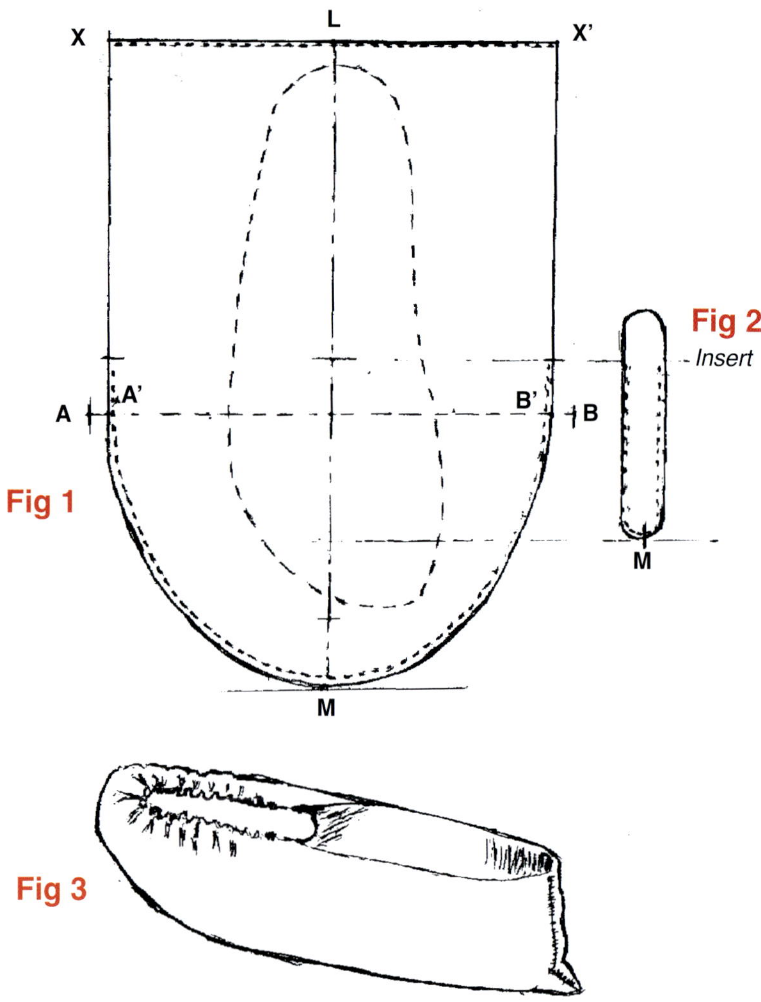

Iroquoian

Medium Insert - Tongue Square Heel

1. See General Instructions.
2. **A B** = circumference of foot.
3. **A' B'**+insert (**Fig. 1 and 2**) = **A B**.
4. **L M** is length of leather from heel and around and up to base of big toe nail. See **Fig. G-3A**, page 21.
5. Sew inside out if the leather is light weight. Sew outside out if leather is heavy.
6. Place insert **M** on sole **M**. Use 1/8" stitch on insert piece and use 1/4" stitch on sole piece.
7. Sew from **M** to point beyond **A** or **B**.
8. The foot opening remaining should be 1/2 the length of finished moccasin.
9. If the moccasin is inside out, bring **X** and **X'** together and sew from **X X'** to **L**.
10. Turn moccasin right side out.
11. This heel is square with a heel tab. See Heel Details on page 24.
12. Cuffs may be added if desired.

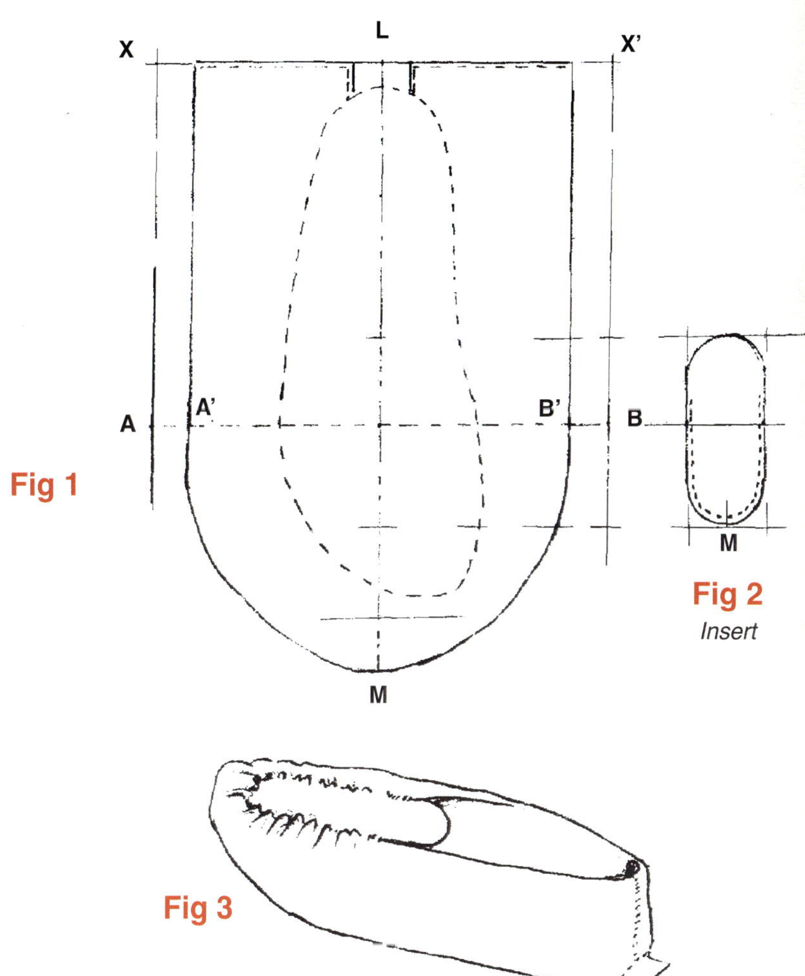

Fig 1

Fig 2
Insert

Fig 3

Iroquoian

Full Insert Tongue - No Heel Tab

1. See General Instructions.

2. A B = circumference of foot.

3. A'B'+ insert (**Fig. 1 and 2**) = **A B**.

4. L M is length of leather from heel and around and up to base of big toe nail. See **Fig. G-3A**, page 21.

5. Sew inside out if the leather is light weight. Sew outside out if leather is heavy.

6. Place insert **M** on sole **M**. Use 1/8" stitch on insert piece and use 1/4" stitch on sole piece.

7. Sew from **M** to point beyond **A** or **B**.

8. The foot opening remaining should be 1/2 the length of finished moccasin.

9. If the moccasin is inside out, bring **X** and **X'** together and sew from **X X'** to **L**.

10. Turn moccasin right side out.

11. Heel seam is a "T" seam. Note heel tab has been cut off. See Heel Details on page 24.

12. Cuffs may be added if desired.

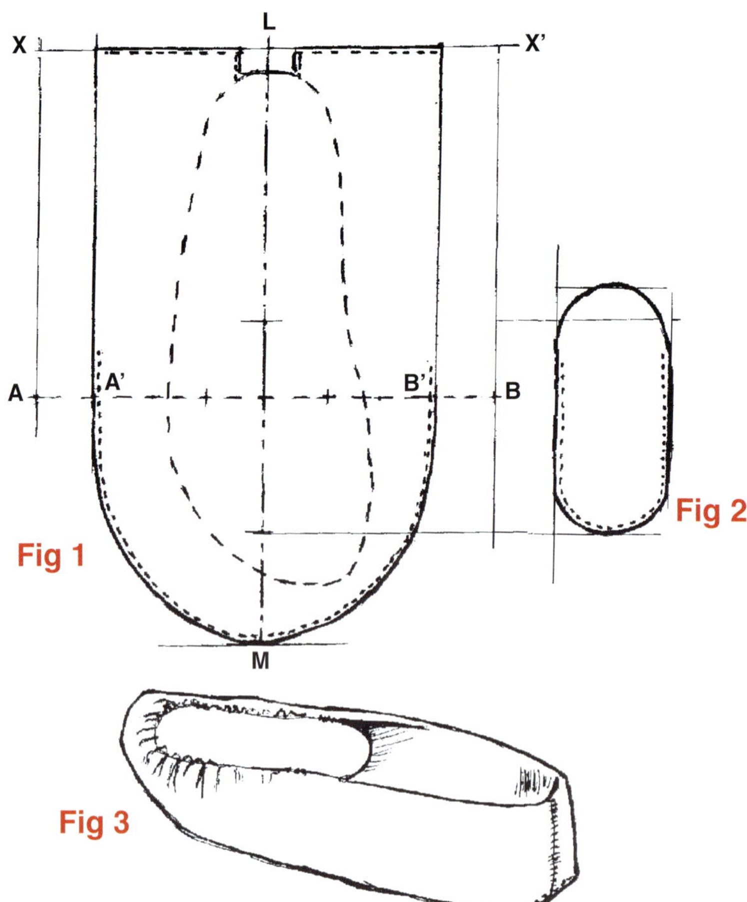

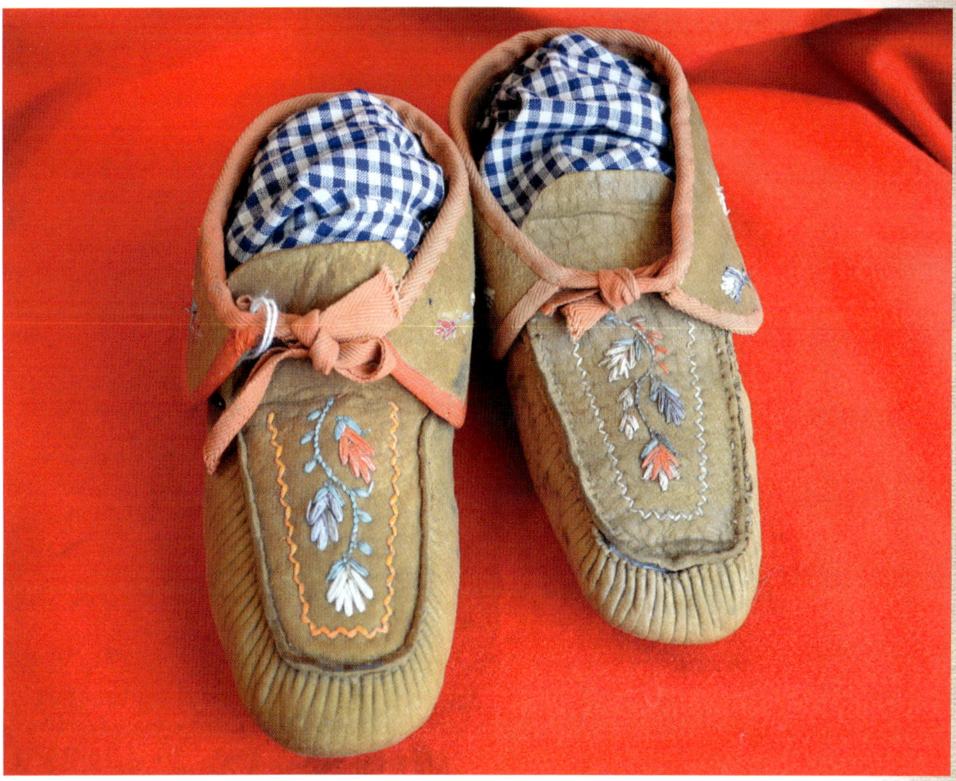

Huron-Wendat Moccasins of the "Full Insert Tongue" type. *Made of smoked, brain-tanned buckskin, moosehair and commerical braid. Note the fine, even gathering stitches used and the moose hair embroidery decoration on the insert vamp and cuffs.*

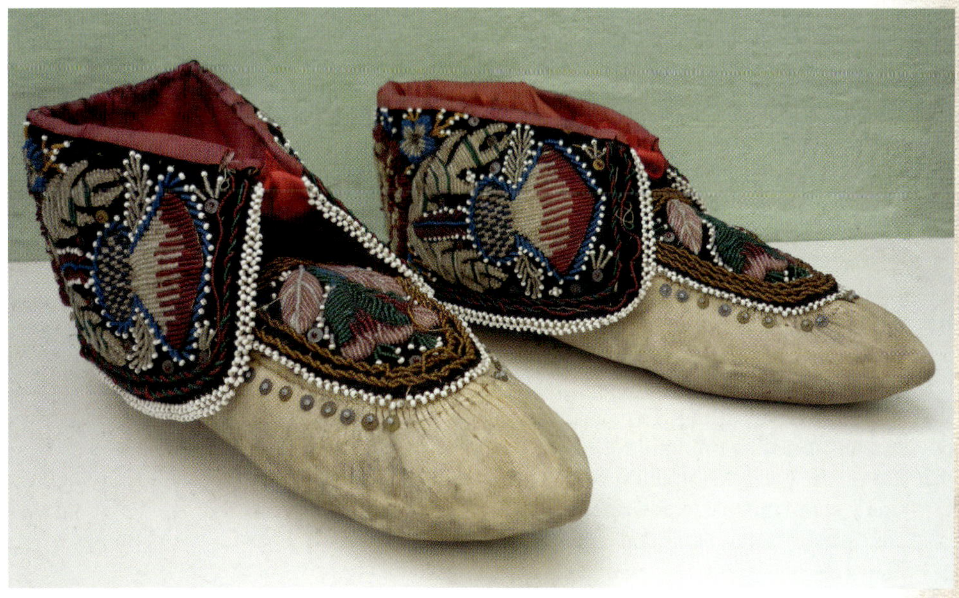

Moccasins, Northeastern Woodlands Haudenosaunee (Iroquois), circa 1840. *Native leather, velveteen, glass beads, metal sequins, silk, cotton thread Vamp construction with puckered toes. Thistle design on velveteen ankle flaps. Richard Green Collection*

The Southeast

Cherokee / Southeastern

Front Seam

The soft sole, one-piece center seam moccasin was the most predominant type among the tribes of the Southeastern United States. The footwear of the Cherokee, Choctaw, Chickasaw, Seminole and Creek is all remarkably similar, with only small variations in construction details. Early examples are extremely scarce, and even non-existent in some cases, but it appears that the moccasins of these were virtually unchanged throughout the 18th and 19th centuries. Everyday moccasins differed from "dress" moccasins primarily in the amount of decoration that was applied.

Moccasins in the 1700s and 1800s were made primarily from brain-tanned deer hides, and even today this is the preferred material. The hides were generally of medium weight, as heavy weight hides do not lend themselves to the gathered seam technique. In order to provide a certain "conditioning" to the leather, hides were most often smoked after tanning, which significantly lengthened the life of a pair of moccasins. The physical consequence of the smoke (and the heat that comes with it) alters the molecular linkages between the fibers of a brain-tanned skin, thus enabling it to be readily re-softened after becoming wet.

1. See General Instructions, page 19.
2. The flesh side of the hide should be used as the inside of the moccasin.
3. A B is the full circumference of your foot at the point you tie a shoe string. **Fig. 1.**
4. L M is the length of your foot plus 1-1/2" (3/4" at front and 3/4" at back). **Fig. 2.**
5. Cuff design was based on individual choice and how the moccasin was to be worn. Apparently this was not associated with tribal style and **Fig. 3A-F** shows six different flap patterns, with **3A** being the classic shape that allows the tops to be worn up for ankle protection or folded down like a cuff.
6. Modify your pattern by choosing a cuff style from **Fig. 3A-F**. If your hide is small, the cuffs can be cut out separately and stitched on to the foot section. With a larger hide, the complete moccasin with flaps can be cut out in one piece (recommended).
7. Test your pattern by folding it over your foot and checking for fit along the top of the foot where the sides of the pattern meet.
8. Using your pattern, cut the leather out and mark the holes for the front seam as shown in **Fig 1**.
9. Stitching Options: Everyday moccasins were typically "sewn" by piercing with an awl and then lacing with a thin, but strong, buckskin thong. Dress moccasins should be sewn with a strong cord, heavy thread or sinew, either artificial or genuine using a steel needle. This results in a smoother seam with smaller, close stitches and less distinct pleats along the center seam.
10. Fold on line **L M**, right side out, making sure the moccasin is symmetrical. It can be trimmed
11. Sew or lace the first 11 stitches, beginning at the center of the toe, **M**, using a baseball stitch as shown in **Fig. F**, page 26 and here in **Fig. 4**. After completing the gathering stitches, finish the remaining 1/3 of the seam with a running stitch. See **Fig. 5**.
12. Put on the partly completed moccasin by pulling it fairly snug over the toes. Then stand in the moccasin and check for length by pinching the leather together so it is comfortably snug against the center of the heel. Trim off any excess overlap greater than 1/4" and make the small **"V"** cuts in the heel as shown in **Fig. 6A**.
13. Whip stitch the heel edges together, up from **L** to **X X'**, pulling the stiches gently snug, as in **Fig. 6C**. Stitching may go all the way to the top of the cuffs or it can stop anywhere in between. After stitching, flatten seam by opening it and pressing it flat with your fingers. See **Figure 6B.**. Sew up the triangular flap as shown in **Fig. 6C**.

14. Laces can be added just under the cuff on either side and then tied in a bow in front. Higher cuffs can be wrapped using a longer lace.

15. Shape your moccasin by thoroughly dampening them and wearing them until dry. **NOTE: DO NOT** wet brain-tanned buckskin unless it has been thoroughly smoked and you are sure you will be able to re-soften it.

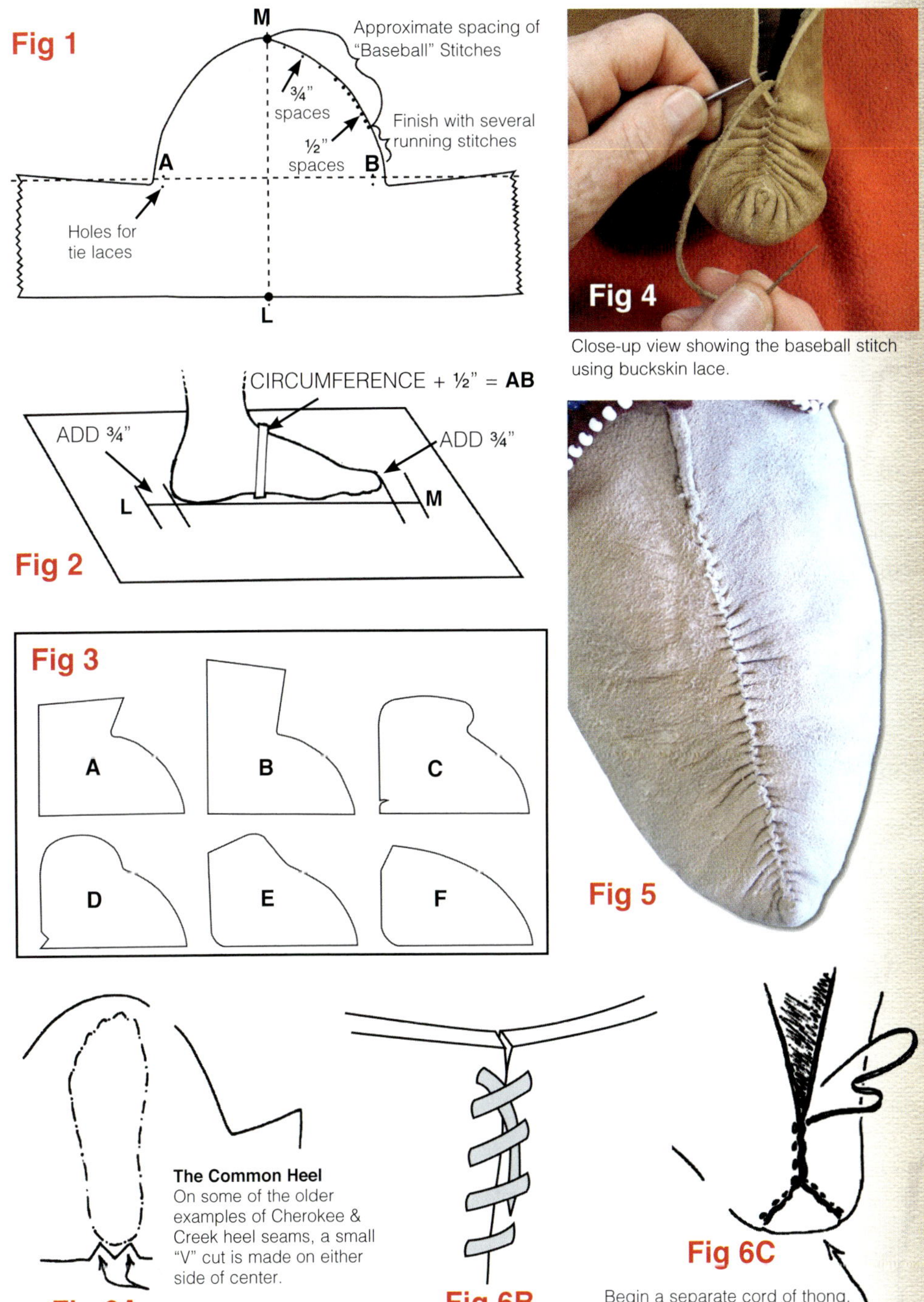

Close-up view showing the baseball stitch using buckskin lace.

The Common Heel
On some of the older examples of Cherokee & Creek heel seams, a small "V" cut is made on either side of center.

Begin a separate cord of thong, then sew the triangular flap into the opening below.

Great Lakes and Prairie

Winnebago

Center Seam

The Winnebago are a Siouan-speaking tribe native to the present-day states of Wisconsin, Minnesota and parts of Iowa and Illinois, and their name for themselves is "Ho-Chunk". They were the dominant tribe in their territory in the 16th century, with a population estimated at several thousand. Before European contact, the Ho-Chunk hunted, farmed and gathered food from local sources, making the best use of the forest and river's resources. With the changing seasons, Ho-Chunk families would move from area to area to find food. Today, they are divided into two federally recognized tribes, the Ho-Chunk Nation of Wisconsin and the Winnebago Tribe of Nebraska, with territory primarily within these states.

1. See General Instructions.
2. Place foot tracing on extra large pattern. See **G-1**, page 20.
3. Note placement of foot tracing. **Fig. 1**.
4. **A B, X X'** and **M** are identical to side seam layout.
5. The flap **X' B2 A2** to **X** is about 1" longer than **L M** length.
6. **J X** and **K X'** may Vary in length but 3 inches is a good length.
7. **A2 B2** will never be longer than **A' B'**.
8. **L' M'** of the flap is center line of flap which falls on **L M** line, after flap is sewn to foot opening.
9. **L' M'** can vary in length. A good length is 1/2 length of foot tracing.
10. Cut pattern on outside line and cut heel. Do not cut the clotted line.
11. Trace pattern on leather, (see **G-4**, page 22), close to edge of leather. Check leather under pattern for cuts, thin spots or holes.
12. Turn pattern over for second tracing so there will be a left and right moccasin.
13. Fold leather along line **L M**. Sew around "T-point" **L' N**. Fold flap around. Bring **X'** of flap to **X'** at heel. Sew from **L' N** to **X'**.
14. Bring **X** and **X'** together, insert 16 x 1/2 inch tie string and sew it at **X X'** point. Sew down to heel cut. See Heel Detail sheet, page 24.
15. Sew across the heel. See **Fig. 2**.
16. The front flap may be worn turned up or turned down.

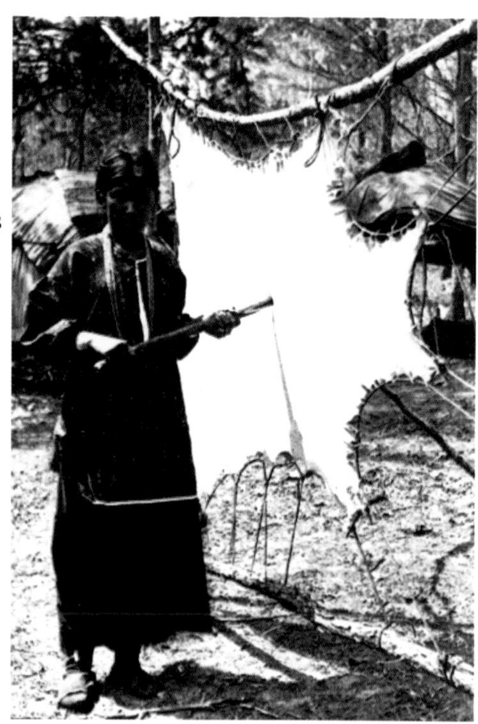

Winnebago woman scraping off meat from a deer skin, circa 1880. Note that she is wearing traditional style, Winnebago women's moccasins that appear to be undecorated.

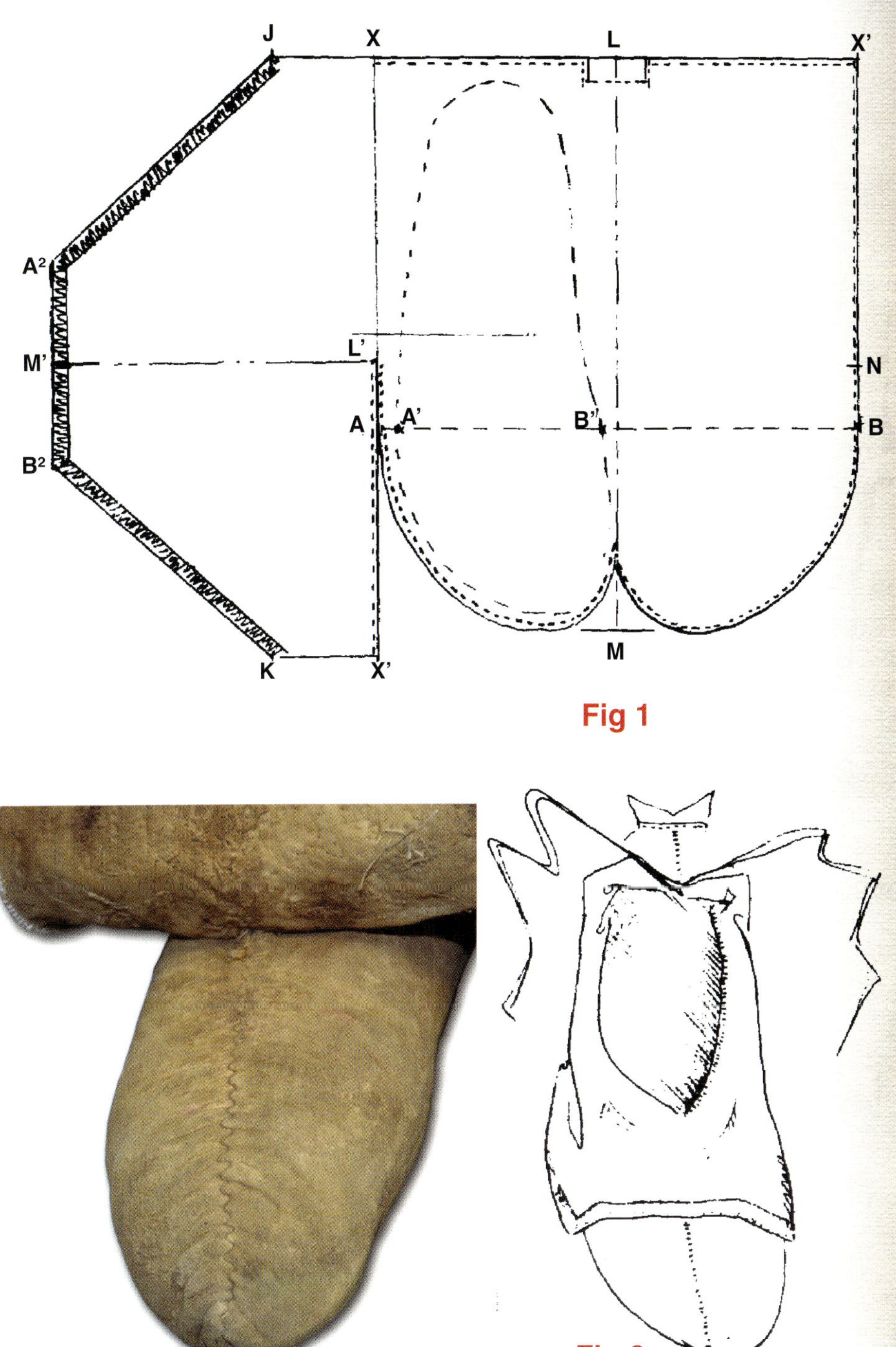

Detail view showing the use of a baseball stitch along the center of the vamp. Courtesy of Detroit Historical Society.

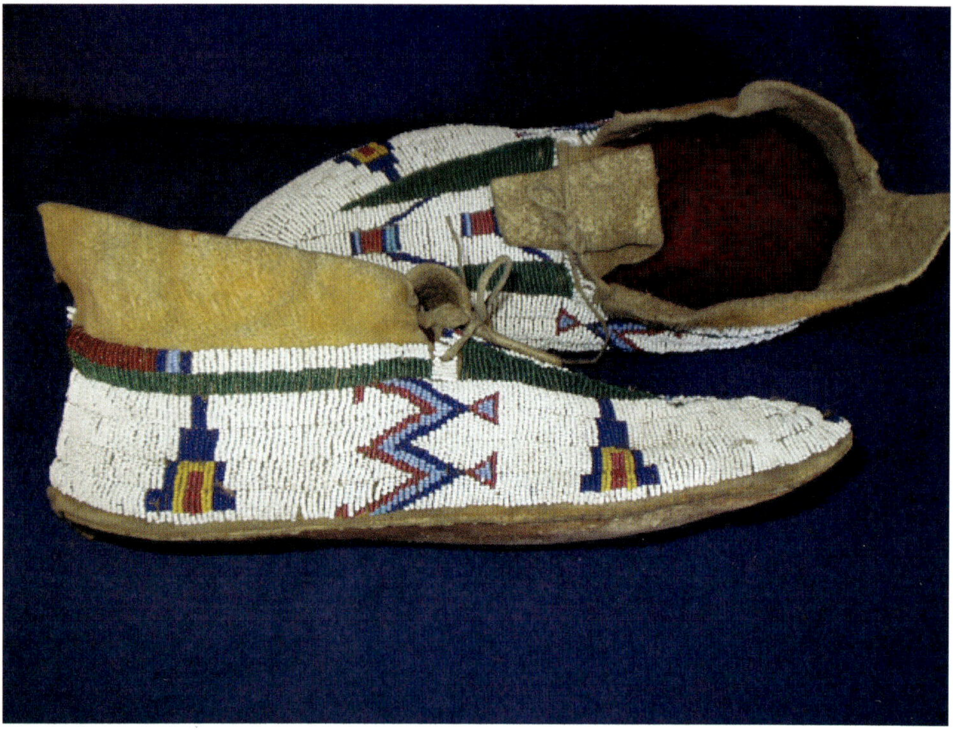

Cheyenne Man's Moccasins, circa 1890. *These classic Cheyenne moccasins include a welt and rawhide soles, and they are fully beaded on brain tanned buffalo hide. Private Collection.*

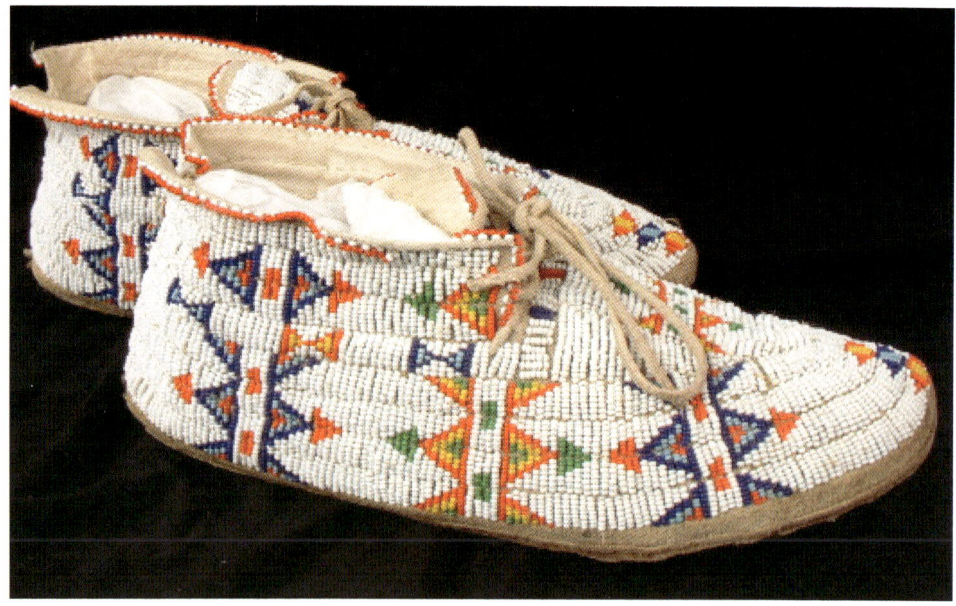

Cheyenne Moccasins, circa 1950. *These moccasins feature beadwork running to the top of the cuffs, which is a feature of later period work most often found in Oklahoma. Private Collection.*

The Plains

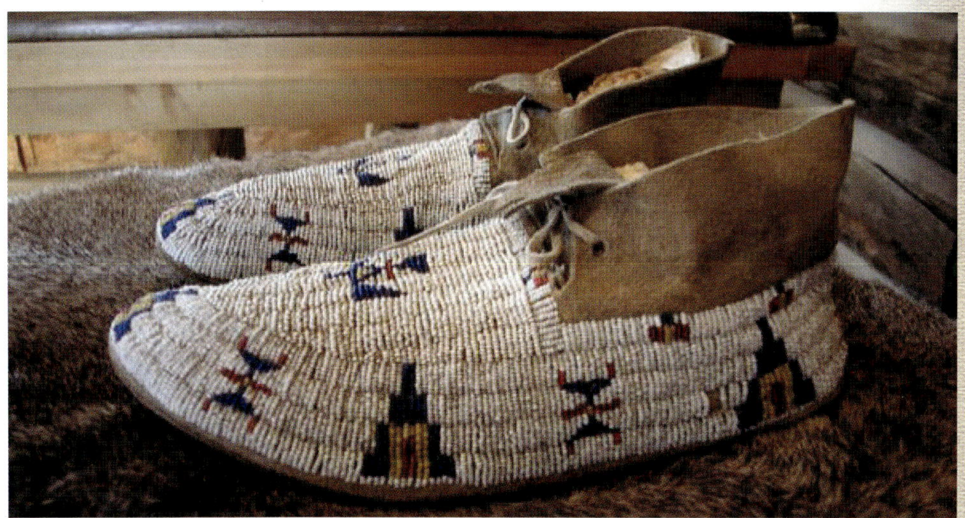

Cheyenne Man's Moccasins, fully beaded, hard soles, circa 1890. *Brain tanned buckskin with rawhide soles and sinew sewn beadwork. Private Collection.*

Plains Hard-Sole Moccasin

Historical Background

The Indians of the Plains wore this hard-sole moccasin which was developed as protection from the hard and sometimes rocky ground of the prairie. Normally constructed of tanned buffalo or buckskin uppers and supple but tough rawhide soles, they represent one of the most highly refined forms of Native American footwear ever developed. This popular style of moccasin is both comfortable and durable for dancing or everyday wear today.

Many styles of construction, decoration, and other more subtle variations, such as tongue style, exist from tribe to tribe. Since Cheyenne moccasin makers have for years been the acknowledged masters of the art, we have chosen to present the typical Cheyenne style of cut and construction.

If you prefer a different tribal style, we suggest researching old photographs and museum examples in order to produce accurately styled and decorated moccasins. See the References section at the end of this book for sources of more information.

Material Requirements

The most authentic and best material to use for these moccasins is smoked brain-tanned buckskin or buffalo. Using brain-tanned hide that has not been smoked will lead to disaster, as it will turn to rawhide the first time that it gets wet. The best commercial leather is German-tanned buckskin, available in both smoked (recommended) and un-smoked types. This is the closest commercial buckskin to brain-tanned, being tanned using a similar process and sharing its desirable characteristics. Other commercial leather may be used, too, but it should be soft and supple. A deerskin of 6-8 sq. feet is adequate for this project. Select hides that are fairly thick and with as few holes as possible. Hides that are extremely thick, however, do not lend themselves to constructing this style of mocassin.

Basic Patterns

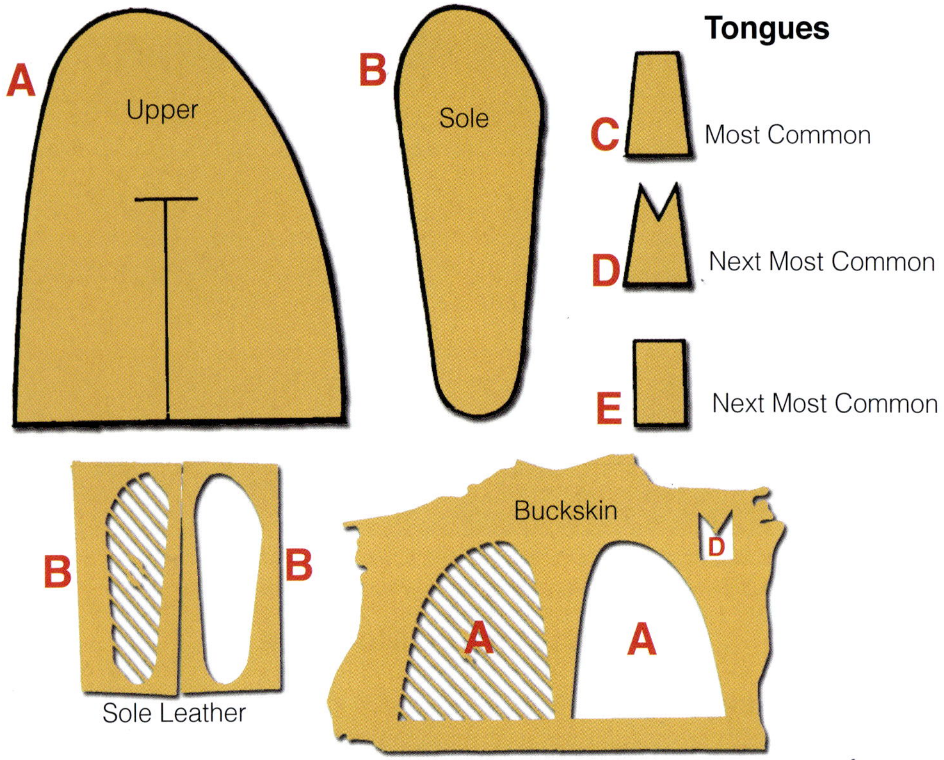

A Upper

B Sole

Tongues

C Most Common

D Next Most Common

E Next Most Common

B B Sole Leather

Buckskin A A D

1. First, draw an outline of your foot on a large piece of paper. Stand with both feet even and your weight evenly distributed. This is more accurate if you have someone help to make the outline for you. Keep the pencil upright and draw your sole pattern as shown in **Fig. 1**, approximately 1/4" to 3/8" longer than your foot. If you do not plan to wear socks with your moccasins, make the sole pattern approximately the same length as your foot. Usually the protrudence on the inside of your foot just behind the big toe is ignored when drawing the sole pattern, and the inside line is almost perfectly straight. In this way the moccasins will form to your foot, ensuring a snug fit. Make a centerline lengthwise down the pattern as shown in **Fig. 2**.

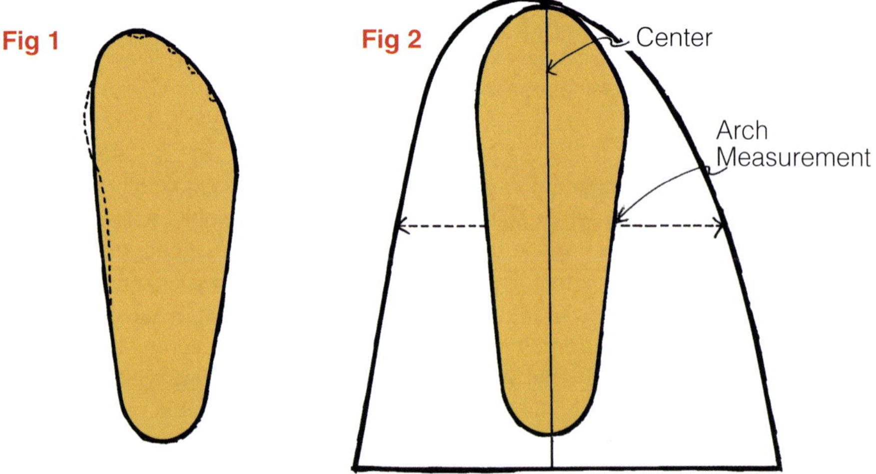

A common tendency when first making moccasins is to cut the sole too wide. We recommend cutting just inside the outline of the sole on both sides. However, this does not apply to the length of the sole! Use the general shape of the Cheyenne sole pattern shown in **Fig. 1** as a guide for drawing yours. Of course, this will vary with an individual's foot shape.

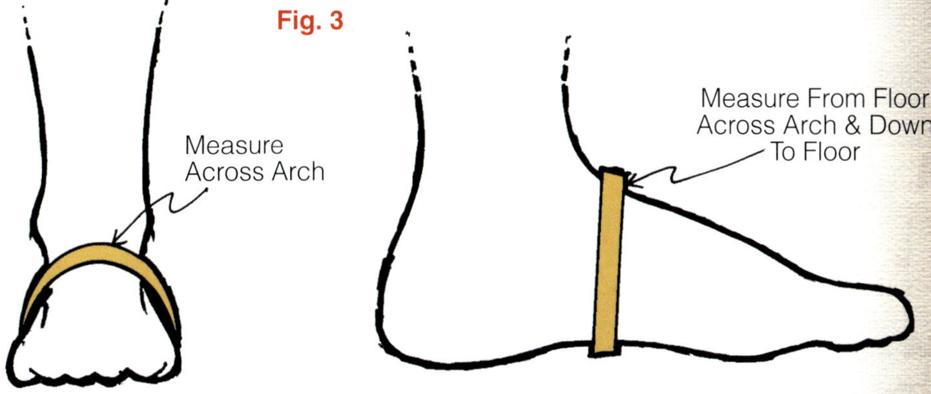

2. To develop a proper upper pattern for your foot, cut a thin strip of paper and measure across your arch at the point where you would tie a shoestring. Measure from the floor across the arch to the floor on the opposite side as shown in **Fig. 3**. Find the middle of this measurement, place this point on the centerline, and transfer the dimension to your pattern. Draw the pattern for the moccasin upper as follows: outline the toe area 1/4" to 1/2" out from the sole pattern. If moccasins are to be fully beaded, allow 1/2" to 3/4". After you draw around the toe, make a straight line through the points for the arch measurement (**Fig. 4**). From these points, continue the pattern sides by drawing lines parallel to the center "T-Cut" line. Continue the pattern at least 1"-2" past the heel. See **Fig. 2**. Starting at the heel, cut the pattern up the center line to the arch measurement (**Fig. 4**). At this point, make a perpendicular cut 2-1/4" in total length (1-1/8" on each side of the center line). The resulting cut forms a tall "T".

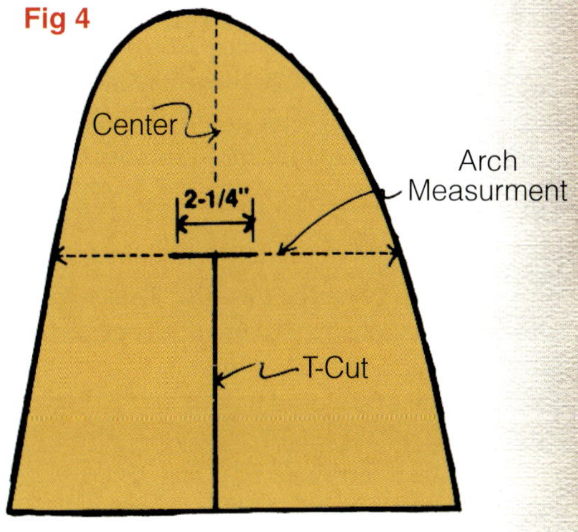

3. Cut out the entire upper pattern and transfer it to your leather, including the T-cut as shown in **Fig. 4**. Turn the pattern over and do the same for the other foot. Be sure to mark the center point at the toe on your leather.

4. Cut out the sole portion of the pattern, transfer it to the sole leather, and cut the soles. Again, be sure to cut one right and one left by turning the pattern over. Then, mark the center point at each toe. Note: the smooth side of the sole leather will be on the outside of the moccasin. When using real rawhide, the hair side will be outside.

5. Any decoration which is to be done to the uppers should be applied now. The beading should begin 1/2" in from the edge and at an angle perpendicular to this edge. This allows1/4" between the beadwork lane and sole, and 1/4" which is used in the whip stitch for added strength of the seam. The accompanying diagrams show typical bead row layouts. After the beadwork is completed, you are ready to attach the upper to the sole by sewing inside-out. The decorative part will be face down while sewing, as shown in **Fig. 5**.

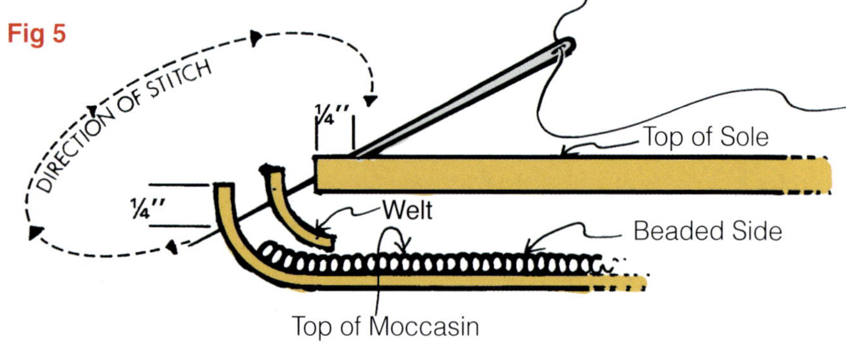

6. Beginning sometime in the 1880's a welt was usually added between the sole and upper of Cheyenne moccasins. This welt protects the stitches and helps keep out dirt, thereby contributing to the life of the moccasin. If a welt is desired (and we highly recommend using one), cut a 1/2" strip of buckskin that is long enough to go around your foot and slightly overlap in the back. Be sure to save enough soft, upper leather for tongues and tie strings.

7. Before sewing, thoroughly soften the leather sole by repeatedly bending it, concentrating especially on the toe area. This is more essential when using genuine rawhide but should be done regardless of the material used. Now, dampen the edge of the sole all the way around, and, using the dull backside of a closed pair of scissors, scrape the edges very hard, as shown in **Fig. 6**. This is an old Indian trick and tends to thicken the edges, thereby making sewing easier.

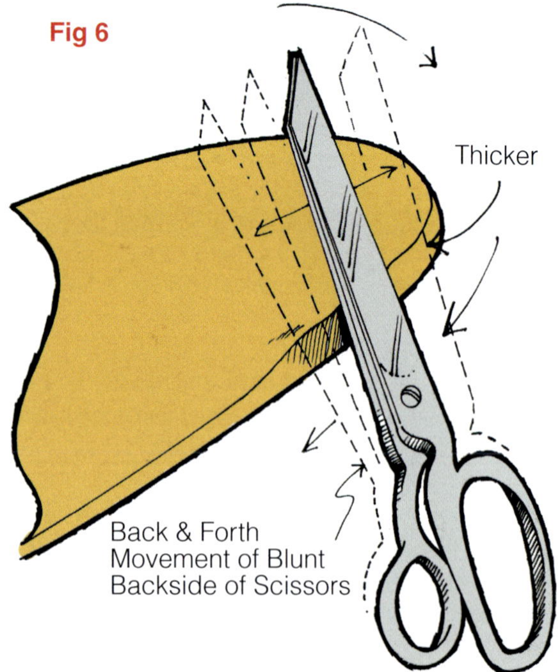

8. Simulated sinew should be used for all sewing other than beading. Cut a 3 foot length and split it in two, then roll it on your leg to make it round. Align the center points on the sole, welt, and upper as shown in **Fig. 7**. Begin at this point and sew two thirds of the way down one side, then do the same on the other side. Use a whip-stitch as shown in **Fig. 5** and 7, keeping your stitches very close together.

Fig 7

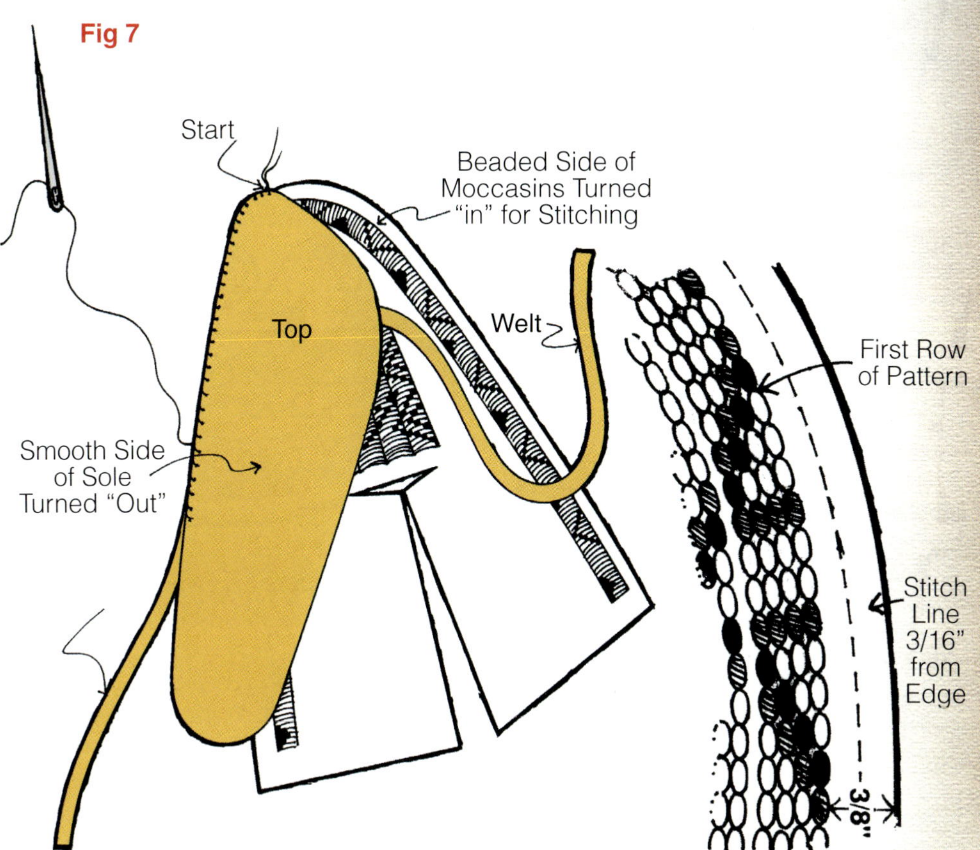

The best Cheyenne moccasins are sewn with stitches that are approximately 1/16" to 3/32" apart, maximum. This gives a very fine appearance and makes the moccasin quite strong. Sewing is facilitated by first piercing a hole in the sole with a thin awl. Pull each stitch very tight so that the welt and upper are snug against the sole.

9. Before you finish the sewing, turn the moccasin right-side-out. Begin by pushing in at the toe and continue by pulling the heel flaps towards the toe. When using very thick, stiff soles, it may be easier if the sole is first dampened with a wet cloth. Avoid getting water on the uppers, especially if using brain-tanned buckskin! This is normally not necessary when using commercially tanned soles. Take your time and work the sole through the moccasin. Next, try on the moccasins.

10. Finish sewing both sides back to the heel. Now mark the leather at the heel where any excess needs to be removed. An easy method is to simply put on the moccasin, hold the leather in place, and crease both pieces of the buckskin up the back of the heel with your fingernail. See **Fig. 8** for a detailed view. Cut just outside your fingernail mark to remove the excess leather. Overlap the two ends of the welt, and then sew up the back using a whip-stitch or baseball stitch. The method of sewing the heel seam is shown in **Fig. 9**. For moccasins that are fully beaded with fully beaded flaps, the flaps should be squared off as shown in **Fig.10**. Partially beaded moccasin uppers are usually not trimmed in this manner.

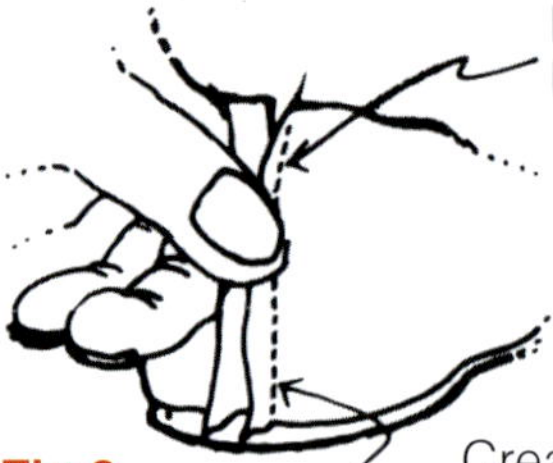

Pinch Excess Leather at Heel

Crease with Thumbnail

Fig 8

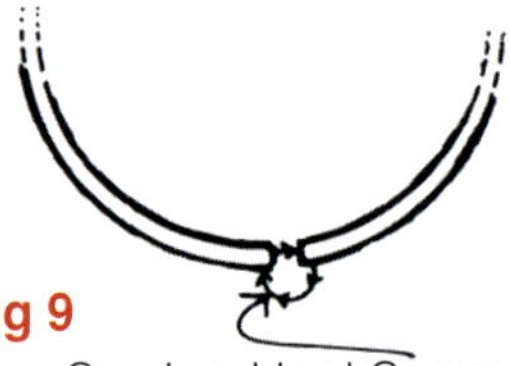

Cheyenne

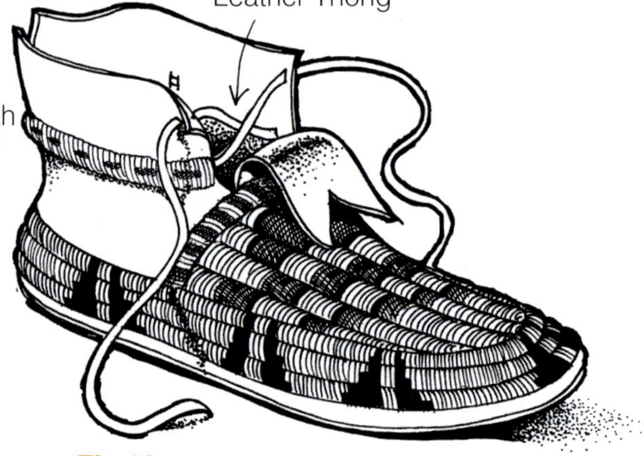

Most Common Method of Lacing Leather Thong

Fig 9

Sewing Heel Seam

Fig 10

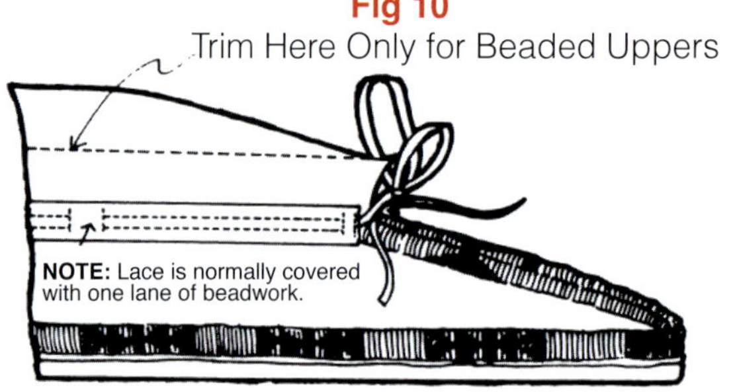

Fig 11

Tongue

Stitch

Stitch

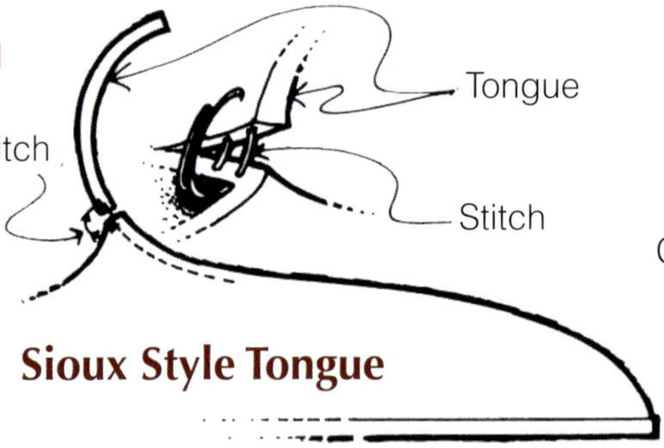

Sioux Style Tongue

Fig 13

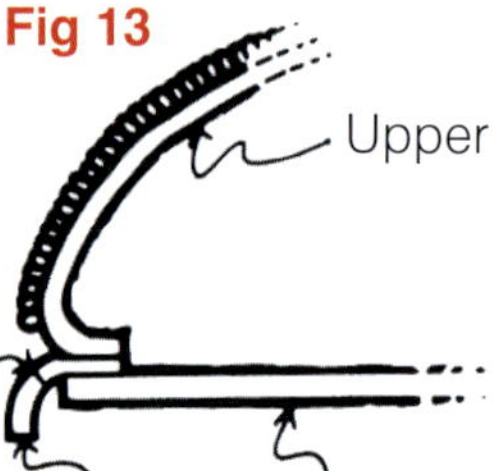

Upper

Cut Welt Here

Excess Welt

Sole

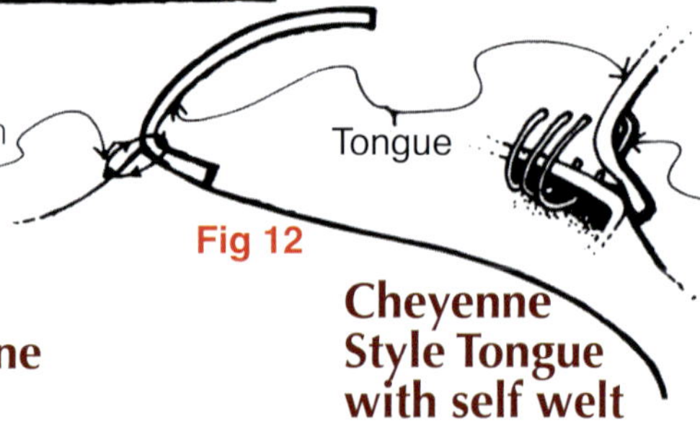

Stitch

Tongue

Stitch

Fig 12

Cheyenne Style Tongue with self welt

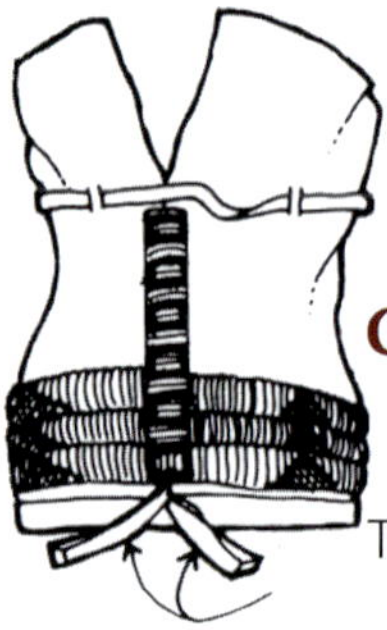

Cheyenne

Tail Left From Welt or Added as Part of Heel Seam

11. Cut two tongues, using one of the styles shown in "Basic Patterns". **Fig. 11** shows the method of attaching the tongues to the moccasins with a whip-stitch. **Fig. 12** shows the common Cheyenne method of attaching the tongue by creating a "false" welt. Cut two thongs long enough for laces, pierce small slits, and then lace up your moccasins. Two methods of lacing are shown in **Fig. 10**. If necessary, the sole welt can now be trimmed to make it even, so fold it down over the edge of the sole and cut it off even with the ground as shown in **Fig. 13**.

Important Note: One of the most traditional finishing touches for Cheyenne moccasins is the two little "tails" found at the base of the heel. These are formed from the two ends of the welt, but on moccasins made without a welt, they are normally sewn on as an addition. Your moccasins are now ready to wear!

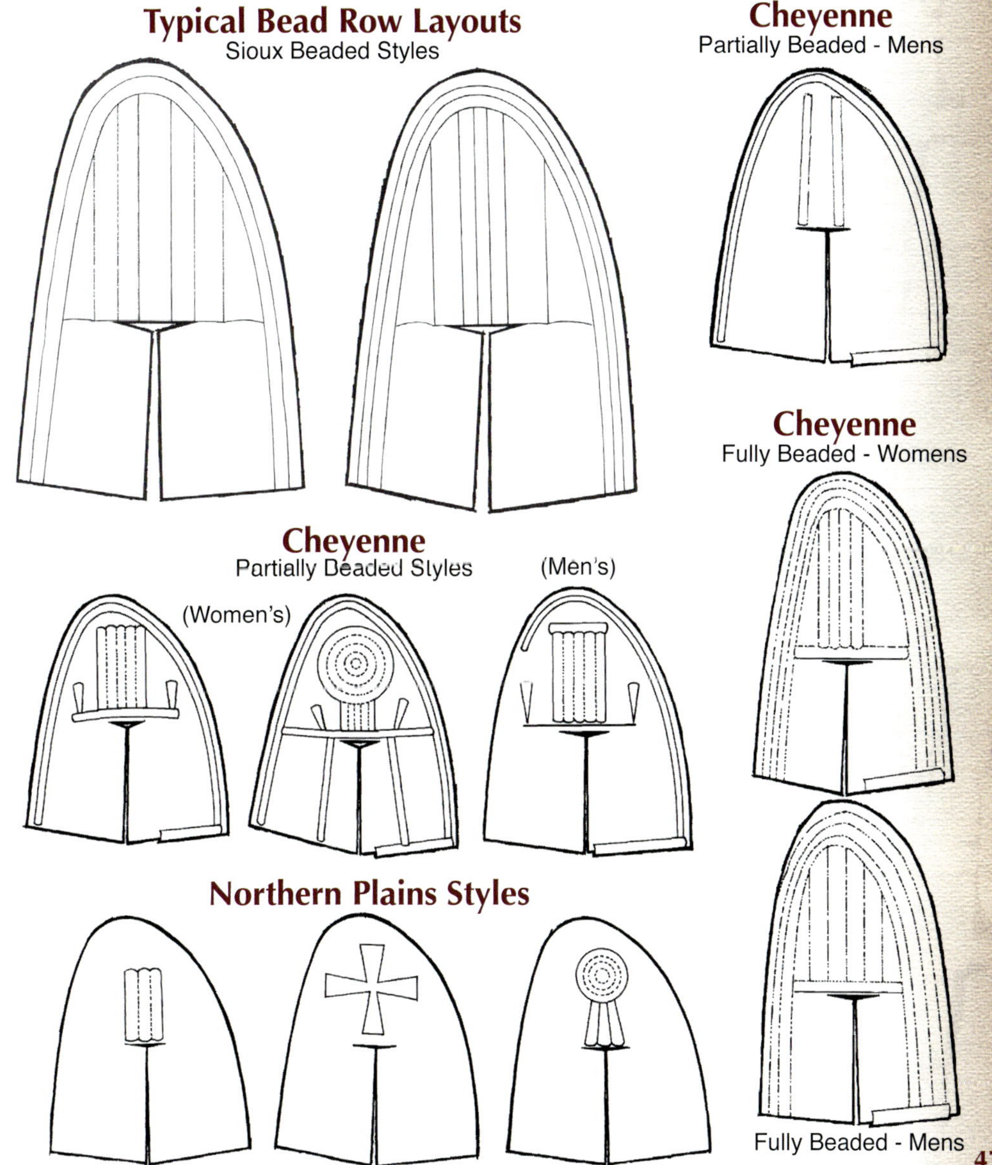

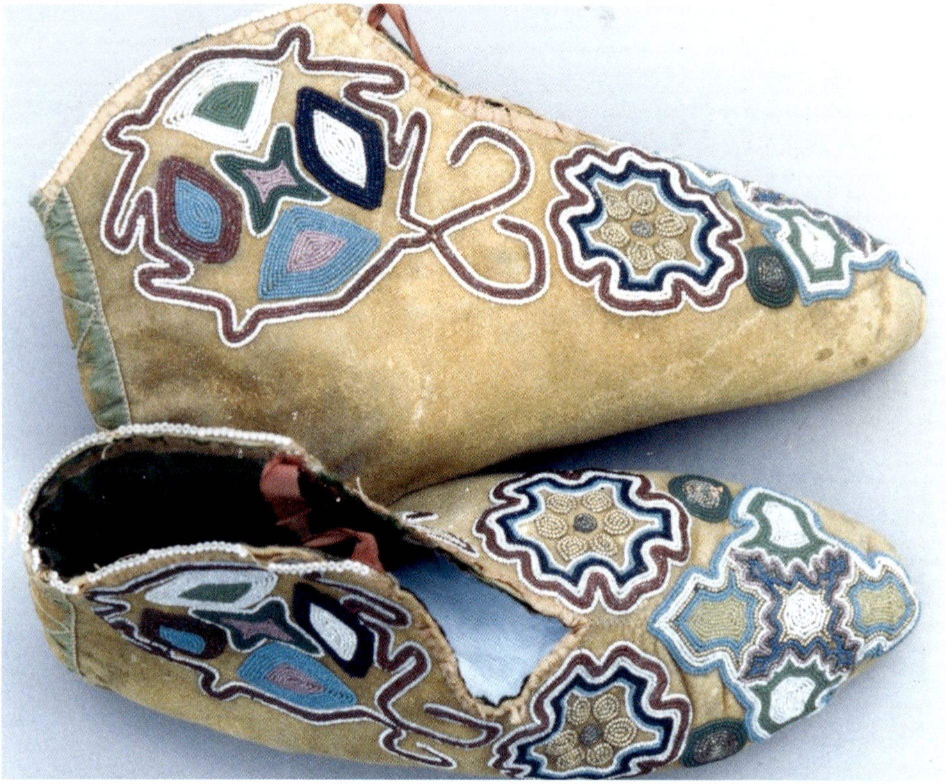

Southeastern Front Seam Moccasins with elaborately beaded vamp and standing type cuffs. *Courtesy of the Painter Collection.*

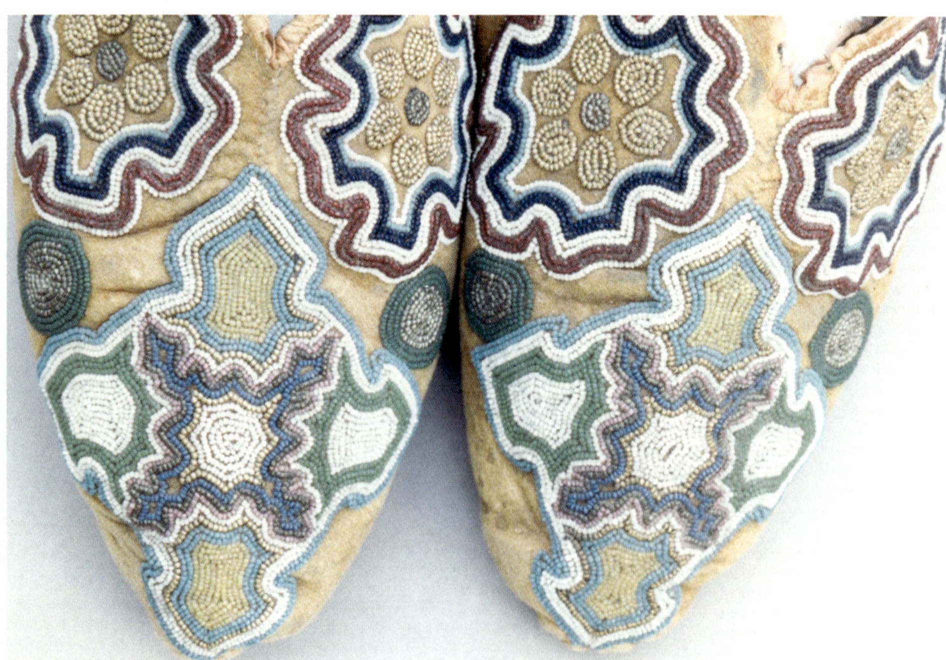

Top view of the fully beaded vamps of the above moccasins showing how the beadwork neatly covers and hides most of the front seam.

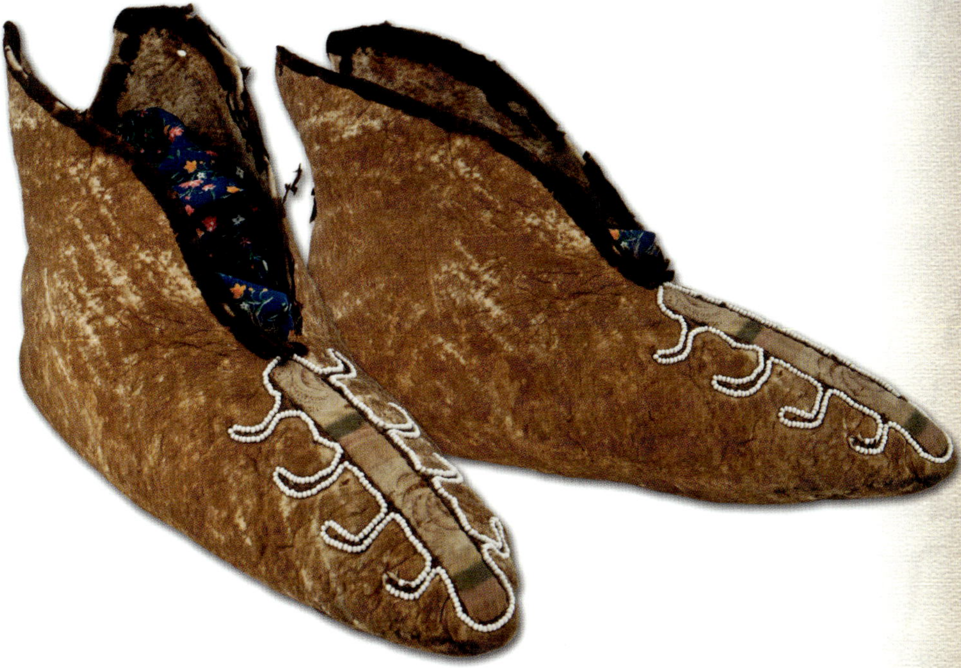

Very early Southeastern Moccasins, circa 1790. *These are the center seam type, with integral, stand-up cuffs and are rather simply decorated using white seed beads, calico cloth, and brown silk ribbon. Private Collection.*

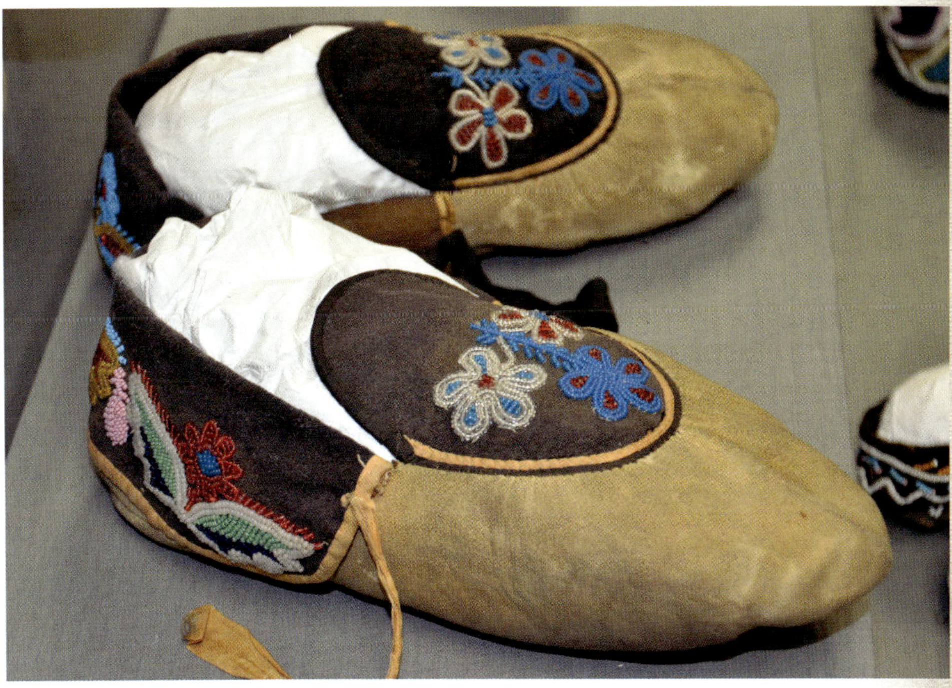

Chippewa Moccasins, circa 1885. *Front seam type with wide insert and large, added flaps. Flaps and insert are covered with black cloth and bound edges, with typical floral bead designs. Courtesy of Detroit Historical Society.*

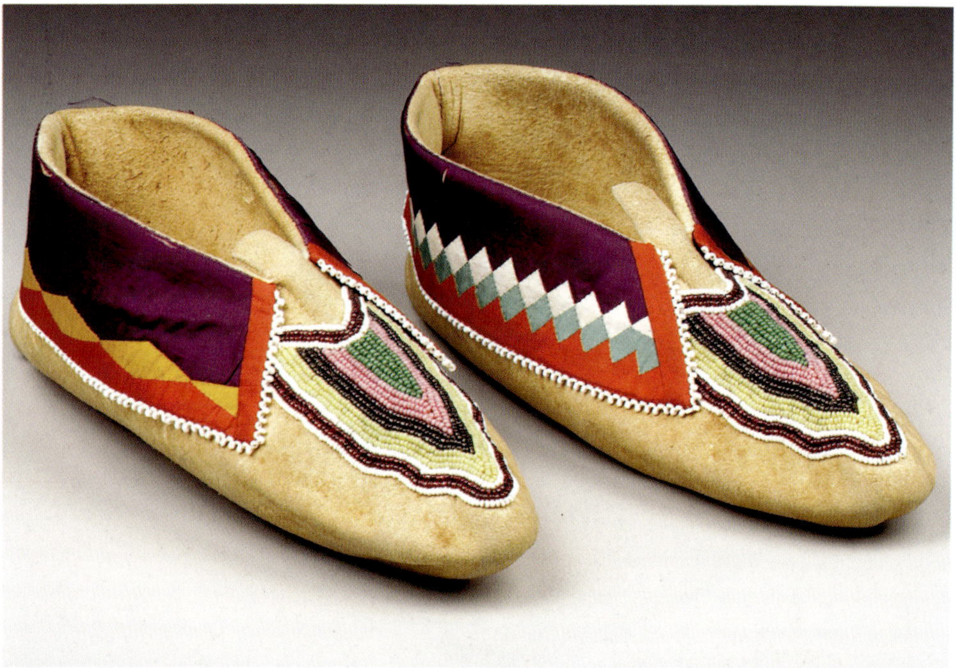

Delaware Moccasins, circa 1900. *These front seam moccasins are made of brain tanned buckskin with very narrow vamp inserts and added flaps. The vamps are covered with applique beadwork in the shape of a stylized "arrowhead" and ribbonwork decoration covers the large flaps. Private Collection.*

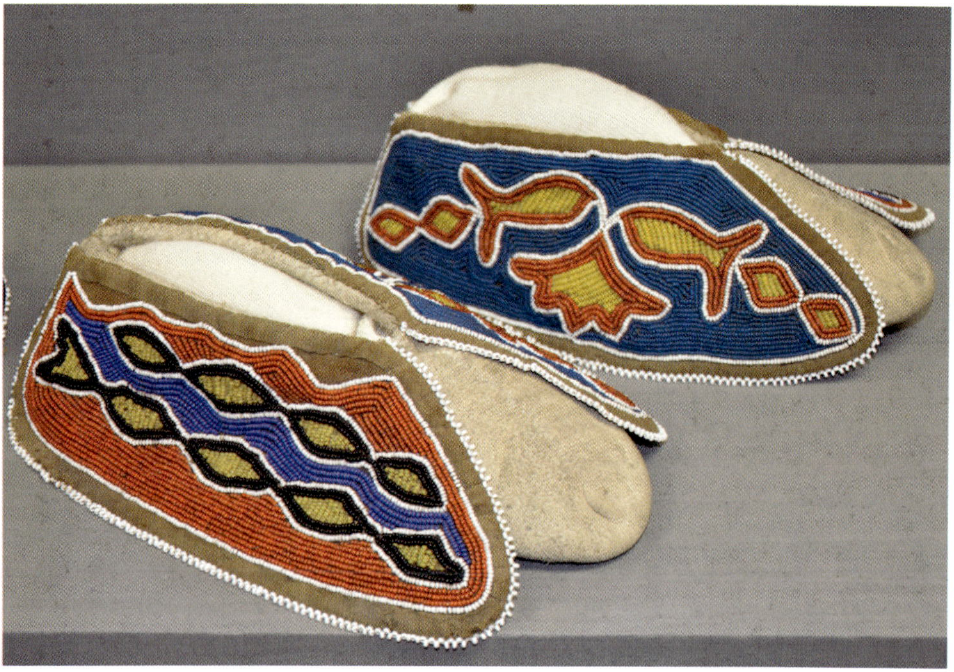

Kansas Potawatomi Man's Front Seam Moccasins, circa 1880 - 1885. *The large, fully beaded cuffs in the applique technique are bound with ribbon and distinguish these as Potawatomi. Courtesy Detroit Historical Society.*

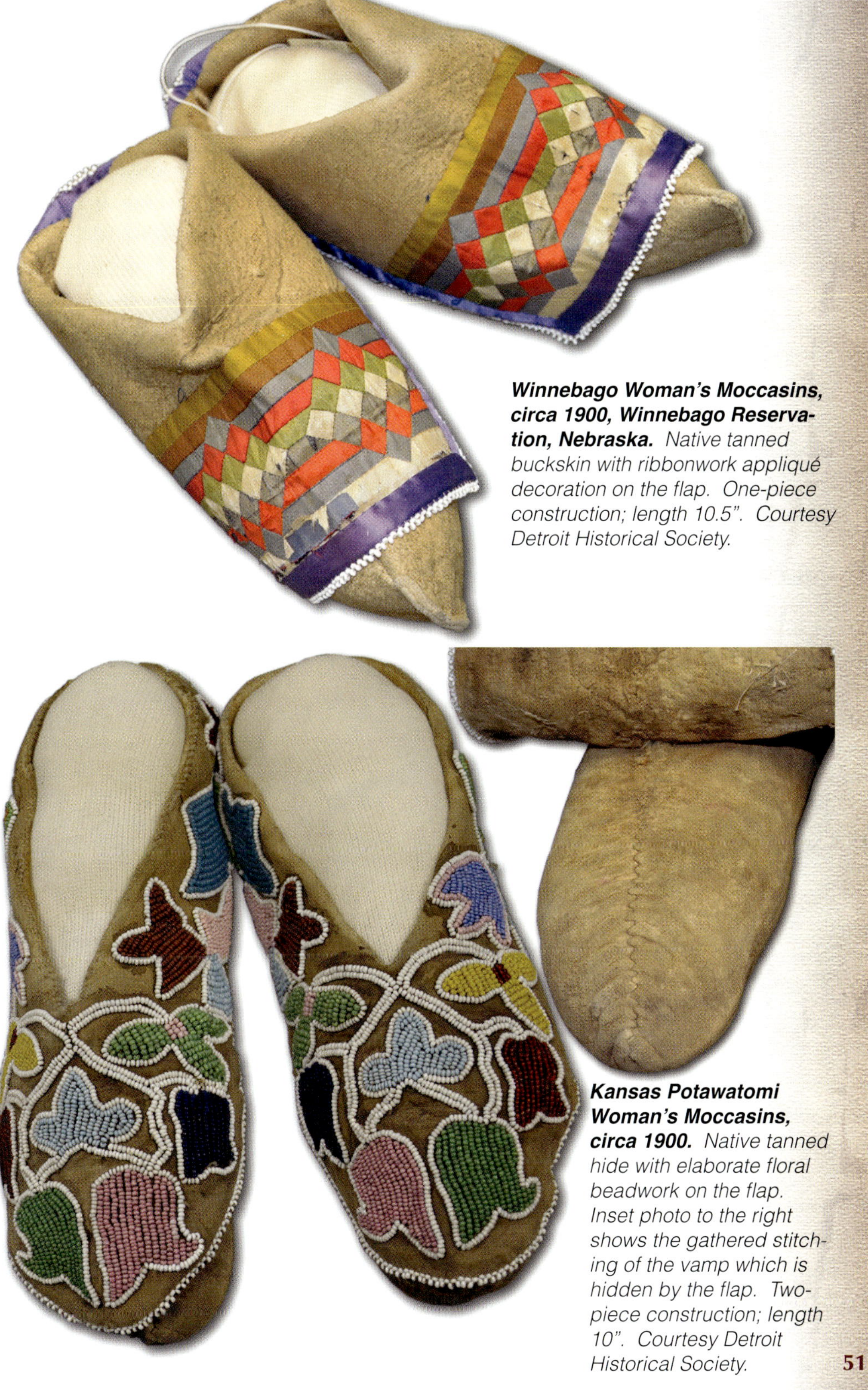

Winnebago Woman's Moccasins, circa 1900, Winnebago Reservation, Nebraska. *Native tanned buckskin with ribbonwork appliqué decoration on the flap. One-piece construction; length 10.5". Courtesy Detroit Historical Society.*

Kansas Potawatomi Woman's Moccasins, circa 1900. *Native tanned hide with elaborate floral beadwork on the flap. Inset photo to the right shows the gathered stitching of the vamp which is hidden by the flap. Two-piece construction; length 10". Courtesy Detroit Historical Society.*

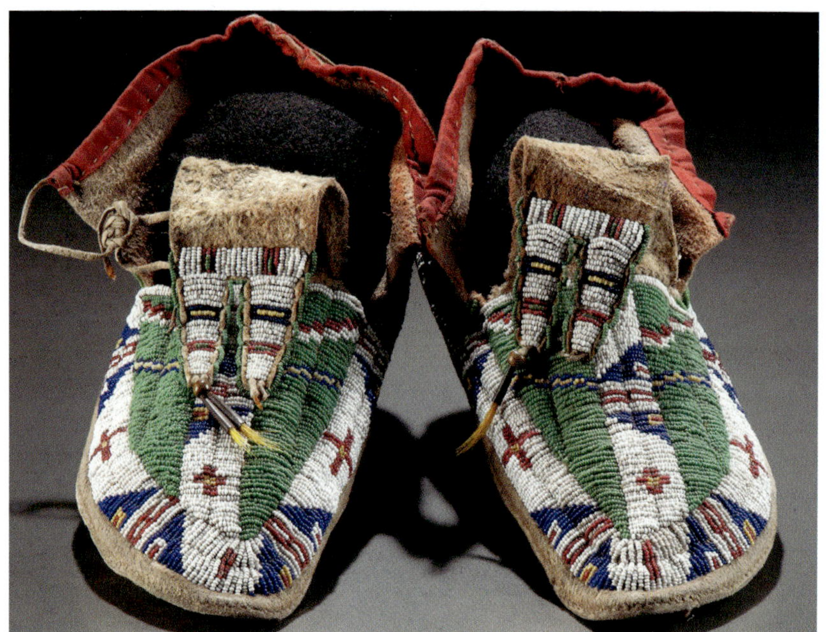

Sioux Moccasins, circa 1890. *Sinew sewn on brain tanned buffalo hide with rawhide soles, these moccasins feature bifurcated tongues with tin cone and horsehair appendages, and cuffs with a simple red cloth binding. Painted designs on the inside of the rawhide soles indicate they are "recycled", being cut from an old parfleche, a common practice. Courtesey of Heritage Auctions, Dallas.*

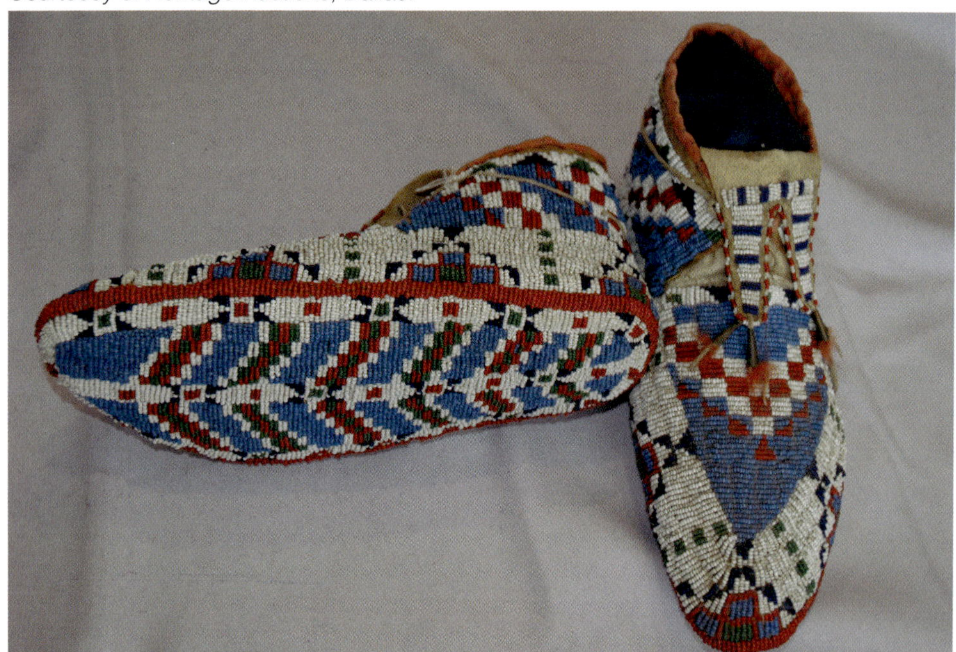

Sioux Honor Moccasins, circa 1890. *Moccasins of this type were often made to show love, honor and respect for wearer and were covered in beadwork, including the soles. Often incorrectly called "ceremonial" or "burial" moccasins, some surviving examples show wear on the bottoms and a few period photos show them being worn, indicating that they were actually used. Private Collection.*

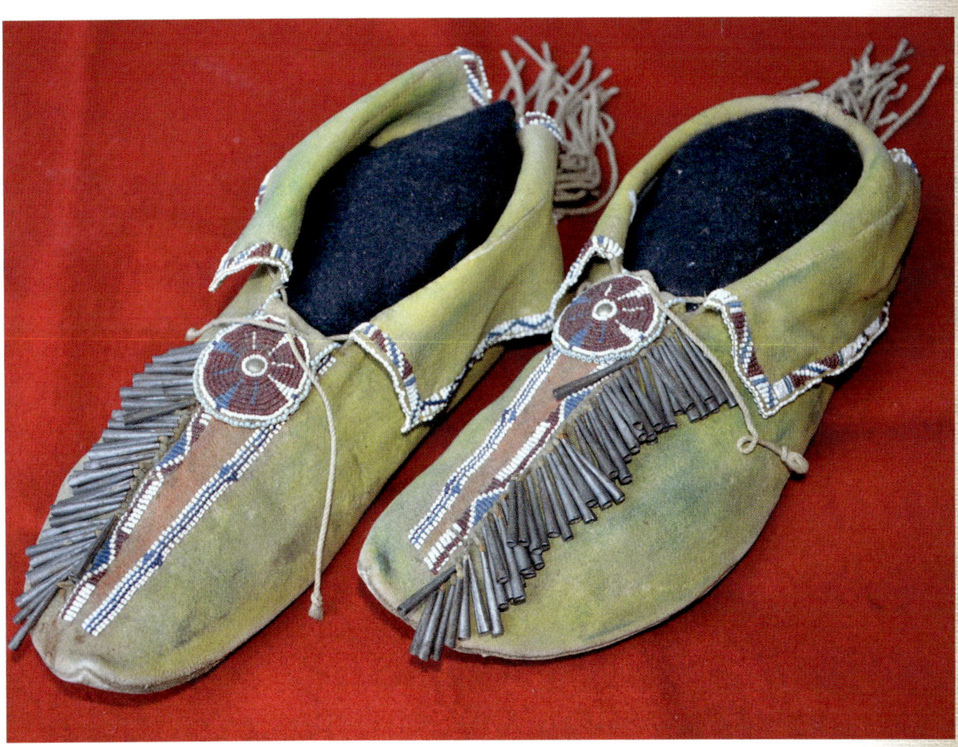

Comanche Man's Moccasins, circa 1890. *This fine pair of moccasins feature native tanned buckskin uppers and rawhide soles, with typical fringe at the heel and tin cones along the vamp. Private Collection.*

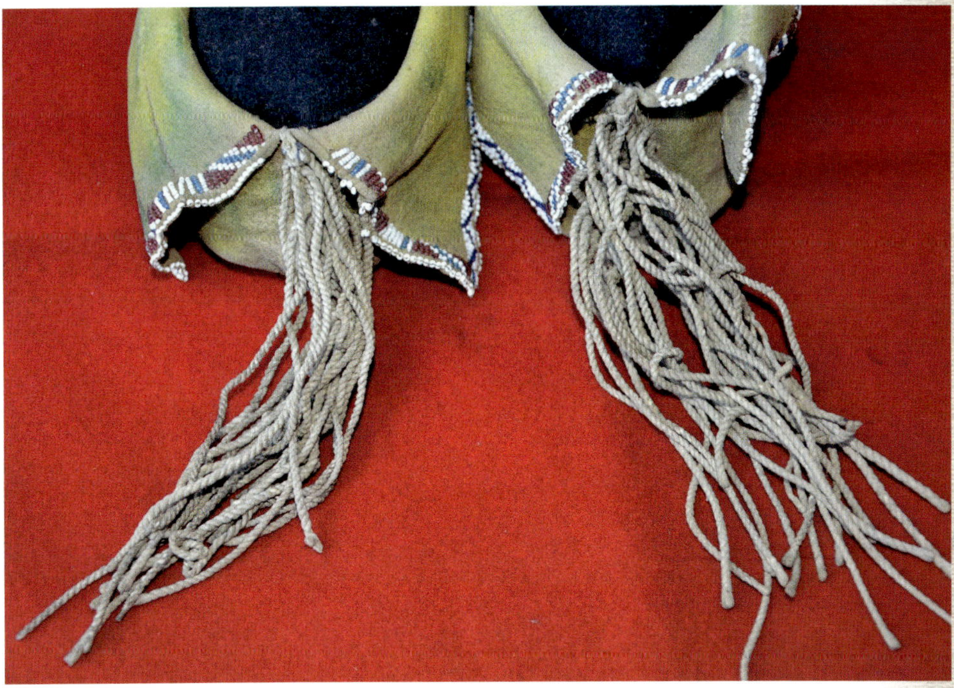

Detail view of the twisted "buckskin" fringe on the above Comanche moccasins. In this case, cotton chalk line material has been used for the fringe in leiu of actual twisted buckskin.

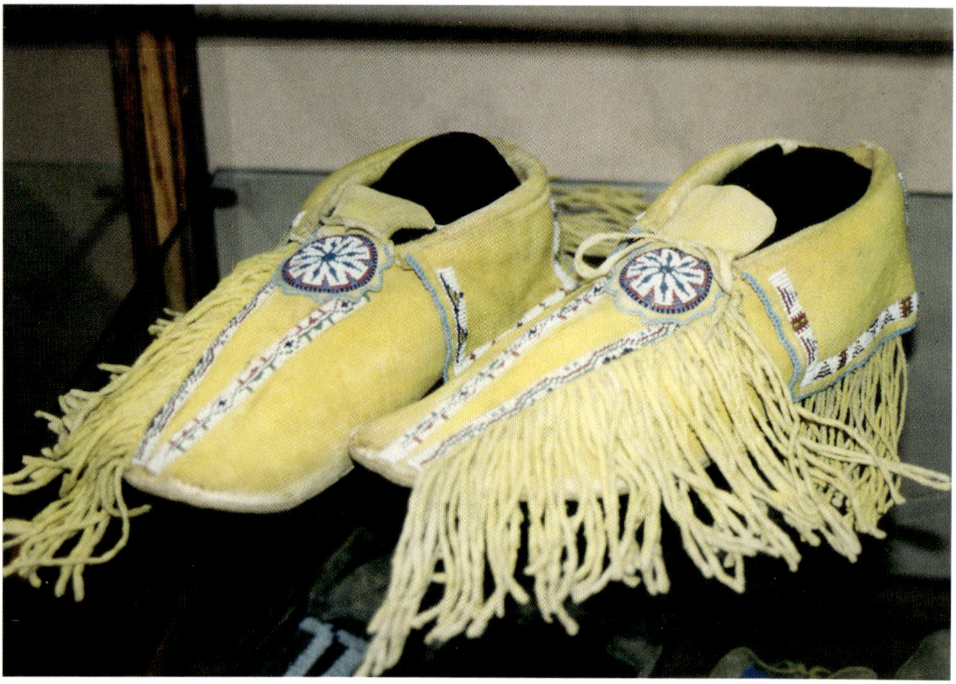

Kiowa Man's Moccasins, circa 1920. *This fine pair of moccasins is somewhat non-typical in that buckskin fringe is used along the vamp instead of the usual tin cones. The flaps are added, as usual and the heel fringe is twisted buckskin. Courtesy of Morning Star Gallery, Santa Fe.*

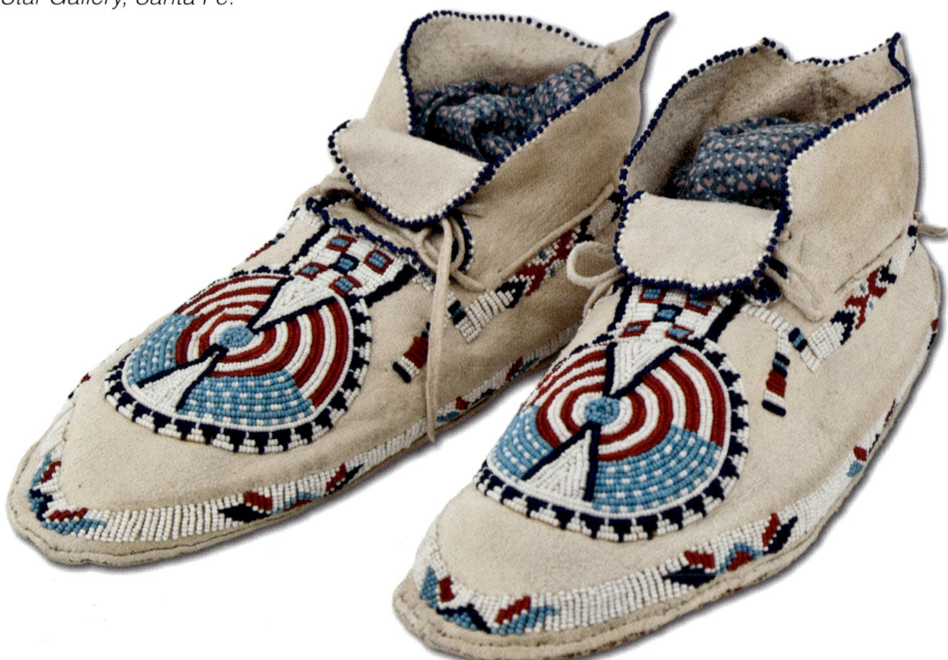

Cheyenne Woman's Moccasins, circa 1960. *This fine pair of women's moccasins represents the finest in mid- to late 20th. century Cheyenne work, using brain-tanned buckskin and hand prepared rawhide. The beadwork incorporates a finely executed American flag motif in 13/0 Czech seed beads. Private Collection.*

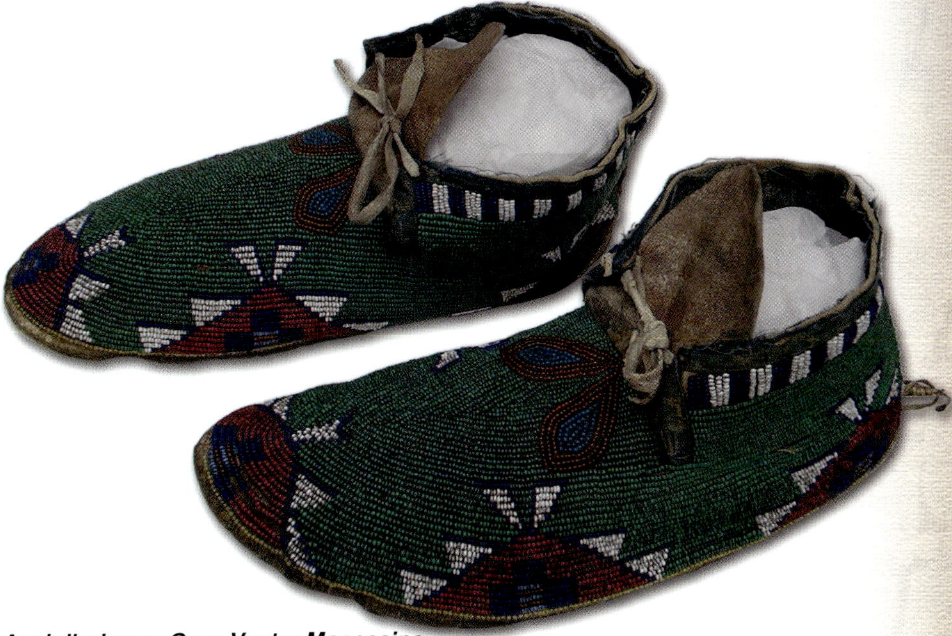

Assiniboine or Gros Ventre Moccasins from Fort Belknap, Montana, circa 1890-1910. *Fully-beaded on native tanned leather, rawhide, glass beads, cotton, sinew. Richard Green Collection.*

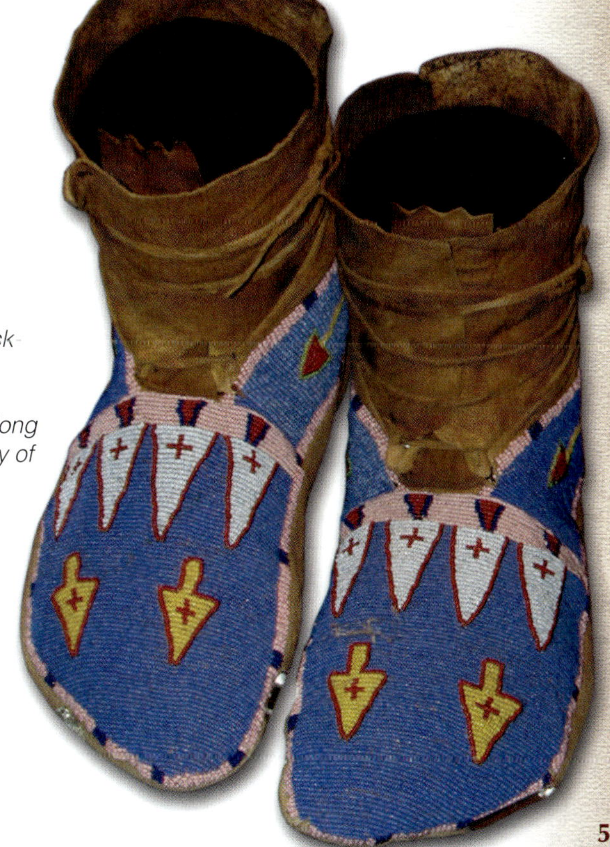

Flathead Moccasins, circa 1900. *Fully beaded on native tanned buckskin, these moccasins feature soft soles and extra long tongues, with high tops that were wrapped with long buckskin ties when worn. Courtesy of Earl C. Fenner.*

Assiniboine

Hard Sole or Soft Sole

Originally part of the Great Sioux Nation, the Assiniboine people occupied the northern Great Plains of the U.S. and Canada. Traditionally, they were semi-nomadic hunters, following the herds of buffalo and hunting on horseback with bows and arrows. Horses were first obtained by trading with the Blackfeet and Gros Ventre tribes, and the Assiniboine eventually became reliable and important trading partners and middlemen for European fur traders and other Indians during the height of the fur trade. Today, they are centered in present-day Saskatchewan, but they have also populated parts of Alberta, southwestern Manitoba, northern Montana and western North Dakota.

1. This design is two pieces; a sole piece and an upper piece. The sole can be made of different leather, such as heavier or half tanned rawhide, or of the same material as uppers.
2. See General Instructions on page 19.
3. Note **A B** plus **A' B'** = circumference plus 1/4" for seams.
4. Make usual foot tracings. (See General Instructions.) Make second tracing for sole pattern.
5. **L M** on this pattern is foot measurement plus 1/2" at heel and 1/2" at toe, because line **M X** is a bit long on this pattern. Draw pattern of foot tracing and cut out.
6. Trace pattern (see General Instructions) on leather. Be sure to turn the pattern over for second tracing as this design has a left and right foot. Cut foot opening **L** to **J K** and cut **J K**.
7. Start sewing by placing leather with the upper centered on line **L M** but even with sole piece. Start at **M** and sew to **X** at heel. Return to **M** and sew second side to **X'**.
8. The tongue is attached and tie string holes are made with an awl. See General Istruc tions. A 12" to 16" tie string is needed. Tops (taller flaps) or fringe may be added. Measure around foot opening and cut a strip of leather about one inch longer than this measurement and about 2-1/2" to 3 " wide. Lay this strip inside even with the tongue piece and use a whip stitch. Sew around to opposite tongue piece. (Be sure to place flesh side to flesh side) When finished the top is folded over outside or pulled up and fringes cut.

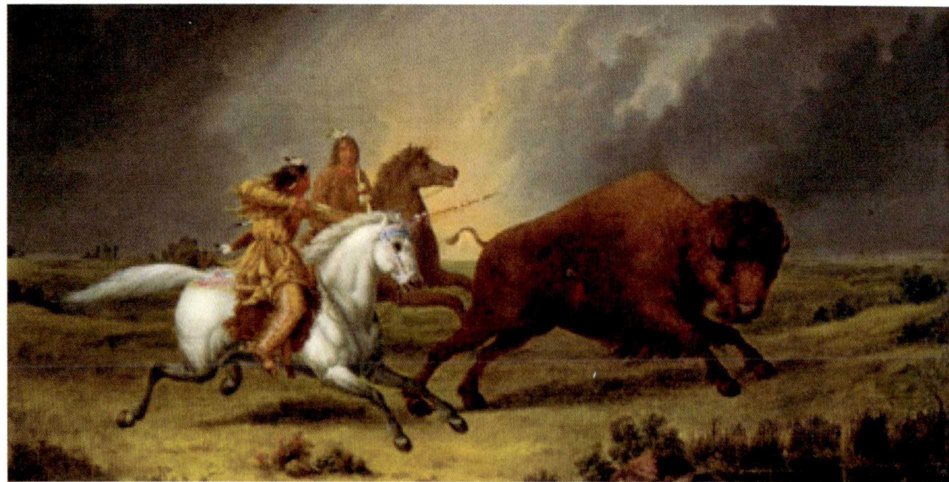

Assiniboine Hunting Buffalo, by Paul Kane, 1851

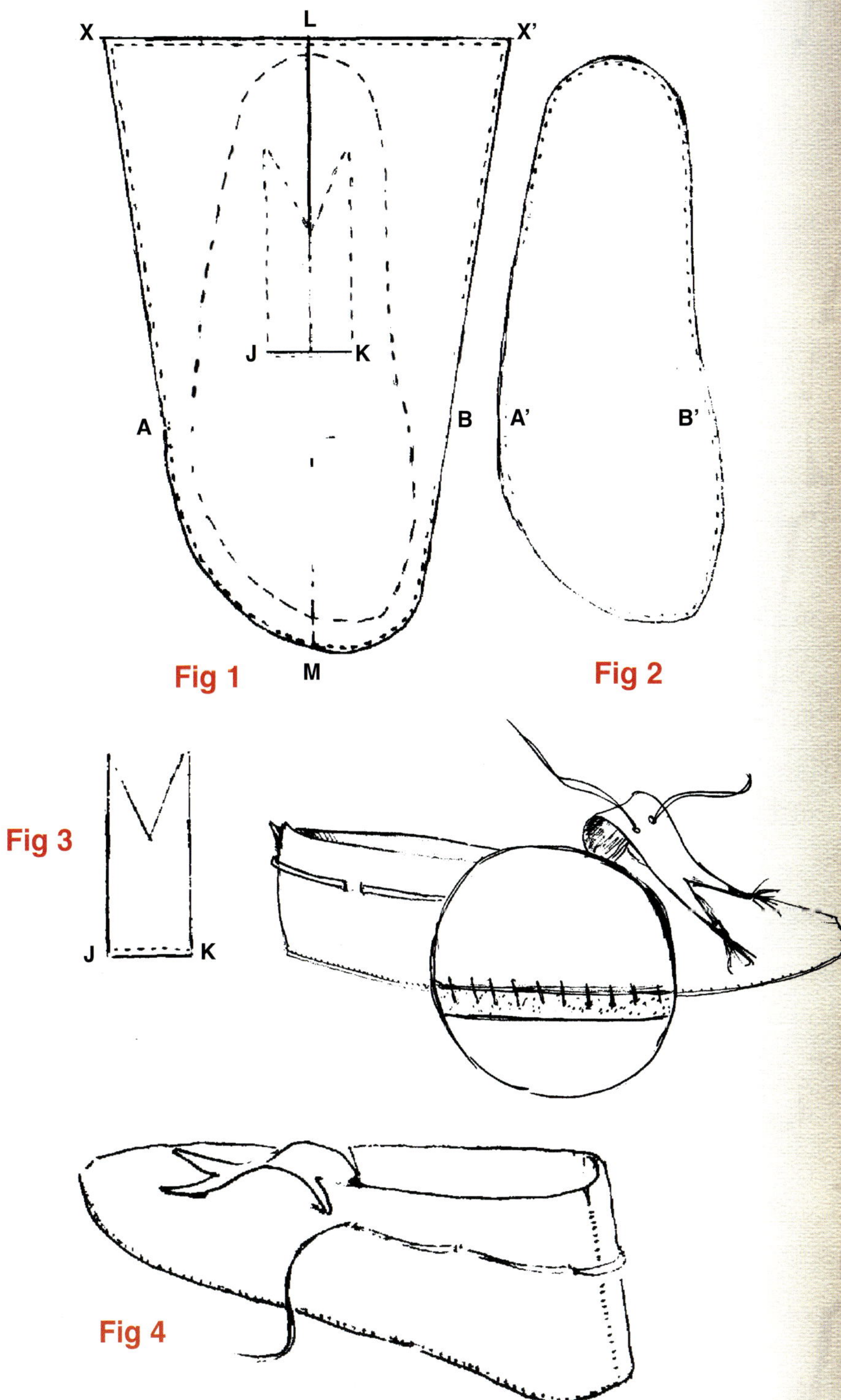
X
L
X'
J
K
A
B
A'
B'
M
Fig 1
Fig 2
Fig 3
J
K
Fig 4

Kiowa-Apache

The Kiowa-Apache, also known as the Plains Apache, are a Southern Athapascan group that, in the late 18th century, lived near the upper Missouri River with their 1780 population at around 400. Later, they traditionally lived on the Southern Plains and were closely allied with the Kiowa Tribe, adopting many traits from the Southern Plains lifestyle of the Kiowa, while remaining ethnically distinct. Today, they are still centered in Southwestern Oklahoma and are federally recognized as the Apache Tribe of Oklahoma.

1. See General Instructions.
2. This design is for a hard sole, but a soft sole could be used.
3. The sole piece is about 1/4" longer than foot tracing.
4. The vamp - upper piece - at points **A' B'** is wider than the sole. When added to sole will be equal to **A B**. See **Fig. 1**. Allow 1 /4" for seams.
5. The vamp - upper extends 2 1/2" to 3" beyond the **L** point, which forms the fringe.
6. Sew toe to heel and as a precaution do not cut fringe at heel seam until the heel is sewn.
7. Sew heel with a double glover's stitch or harness stitch.
8. Note the upper flap is not sewn.
9. **Fig. 3** shows the tongue which is sewn on **J' K'** line to the foot opening, **J K**. Fold the tongue on **J' K'** over **J K** with the square piece up. Use a whip stitch to catch the 3 thicknesses of leather.
10. After sewing pull the square end upright, and put holes in the fringed side of tongue. See **Fig. 4**.
11. The tie-string is about 16" long.

Essa-queta, Plains Apache chief

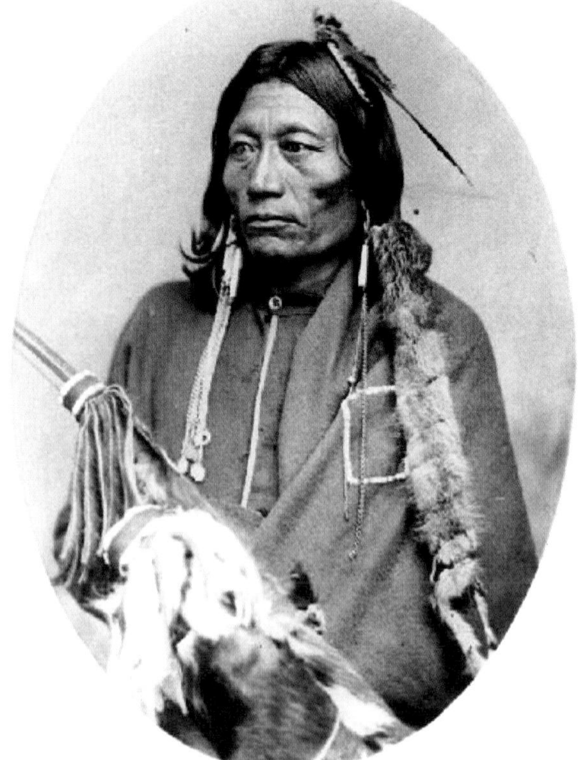

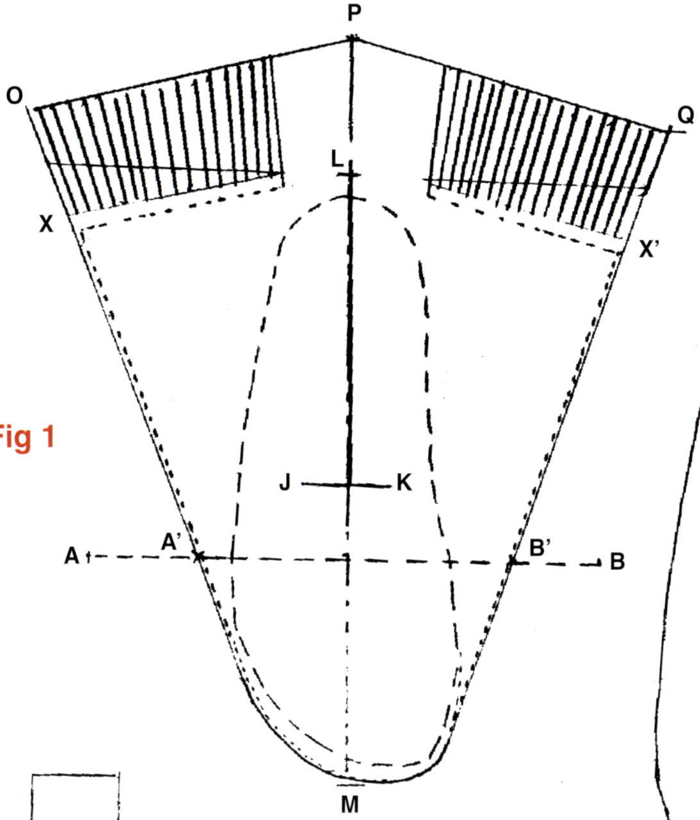

P

O

Q

L

X

X'

J K

A A' B' B

M

Fig 1

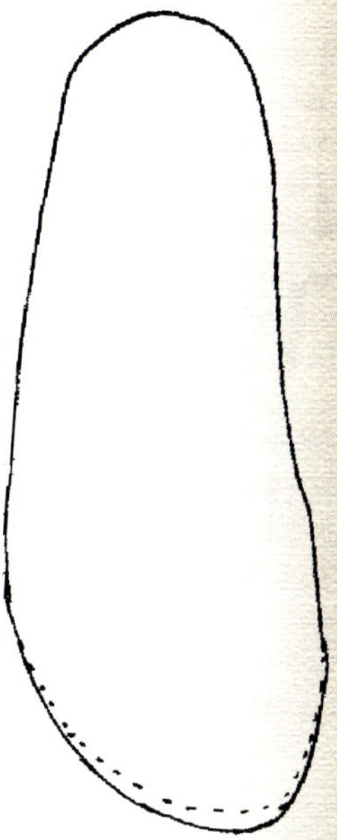

Fig 2

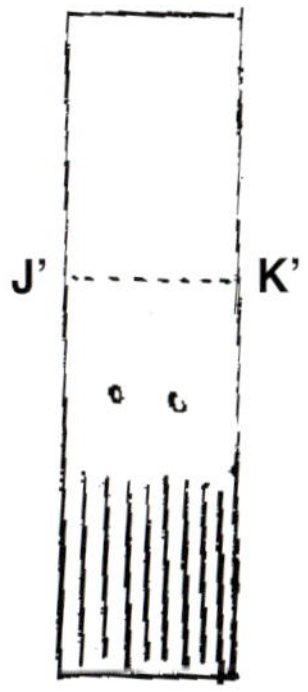

J' K'

Fig 3

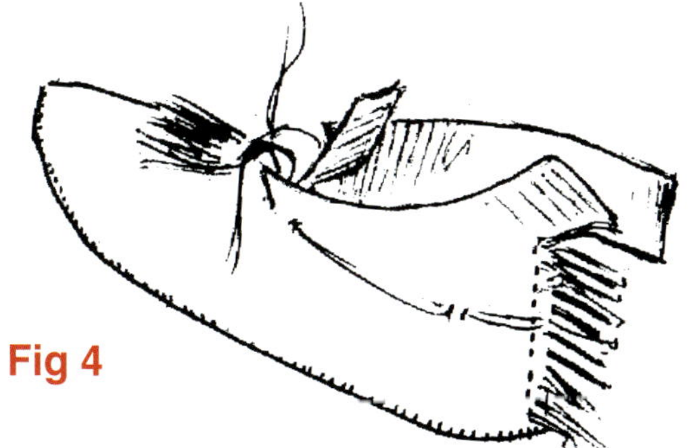

Fig 4

Apache

Shaped-Sole - 3-Piece

The Apache are the southern branch of the Athapascan linguistic family, composed of many sub-tribes that lived in the Arizona-New Mexico region and eastward on the plains of Texas to the western boundary of Oklahoma. Prominent groups included the Mescalero and Jicarilla, now living in New Mexico, and the Chiricahua and Plains Apache who now live in the vicinity of Apache, Oklahoma.

1. See General Instructions.
2. **A B** = circumference.
3. **A' B'** + vamp = **A B**.
4. Note vamp widens at points **J** and **K**, also that **J** and **K** extend beyond mid-point.
5. Note that **J'** and **K'** overlap point **J** and **K**. The overlap is about 1".
6. The sole piece is about 3/4" wider than foot tracing.
7. The vamp is same size as foot tracing over toe but becomes wider at points **J** and **K**. **A' B'** should fit snugly but loosely at points **J** and **K**.
8. Cut 2 sole pieces, be sure to turn the pattern over for second sole.
9. Cut 2 vamp pieces, be sure to turn the pattern for second vamp.
10. Cut 2 back pieces. (See **Fig. 2**. Note the shape of the ends.)
11. Shape sole by using draw string as shown in (**Fig. 1**, page 17).
12. The shaped sole should fit the foot.
13. Sew from **M** to **J**, or **K**. Be sure to secure the gathered sole to the vamp piece.
14. Start sewing back piece at **J'**overlapping **J** about 1". Sew around heel to point **K'**. If **K'** point is too long it can be trimmed before completing the sewing.
15. The tie string is about 16" long.

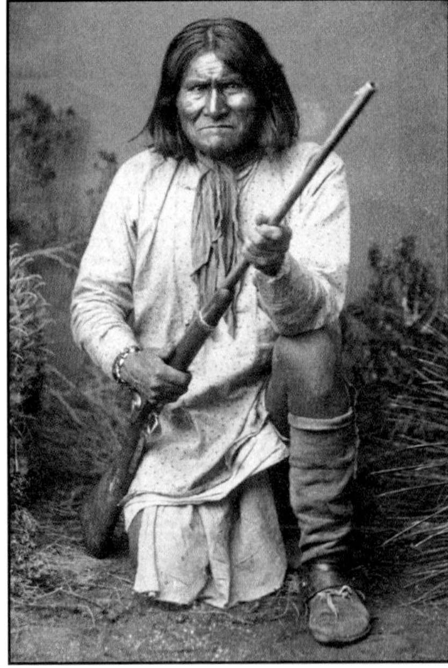

Geronimo, Apache leader wearing high top moccasins with shaped soles.

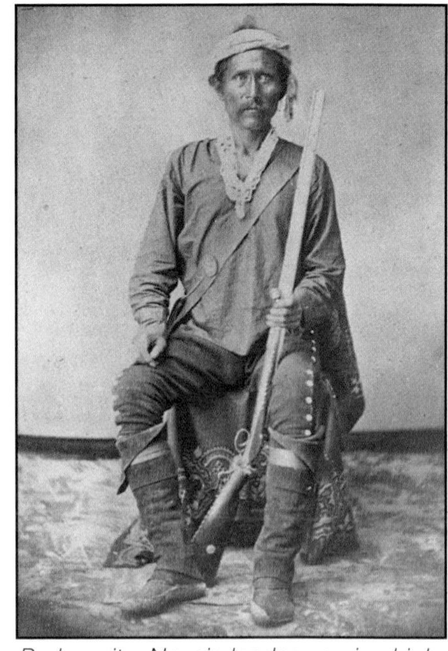

Barboncito, Navajo leader wearing high top moccasins with shaped soles.

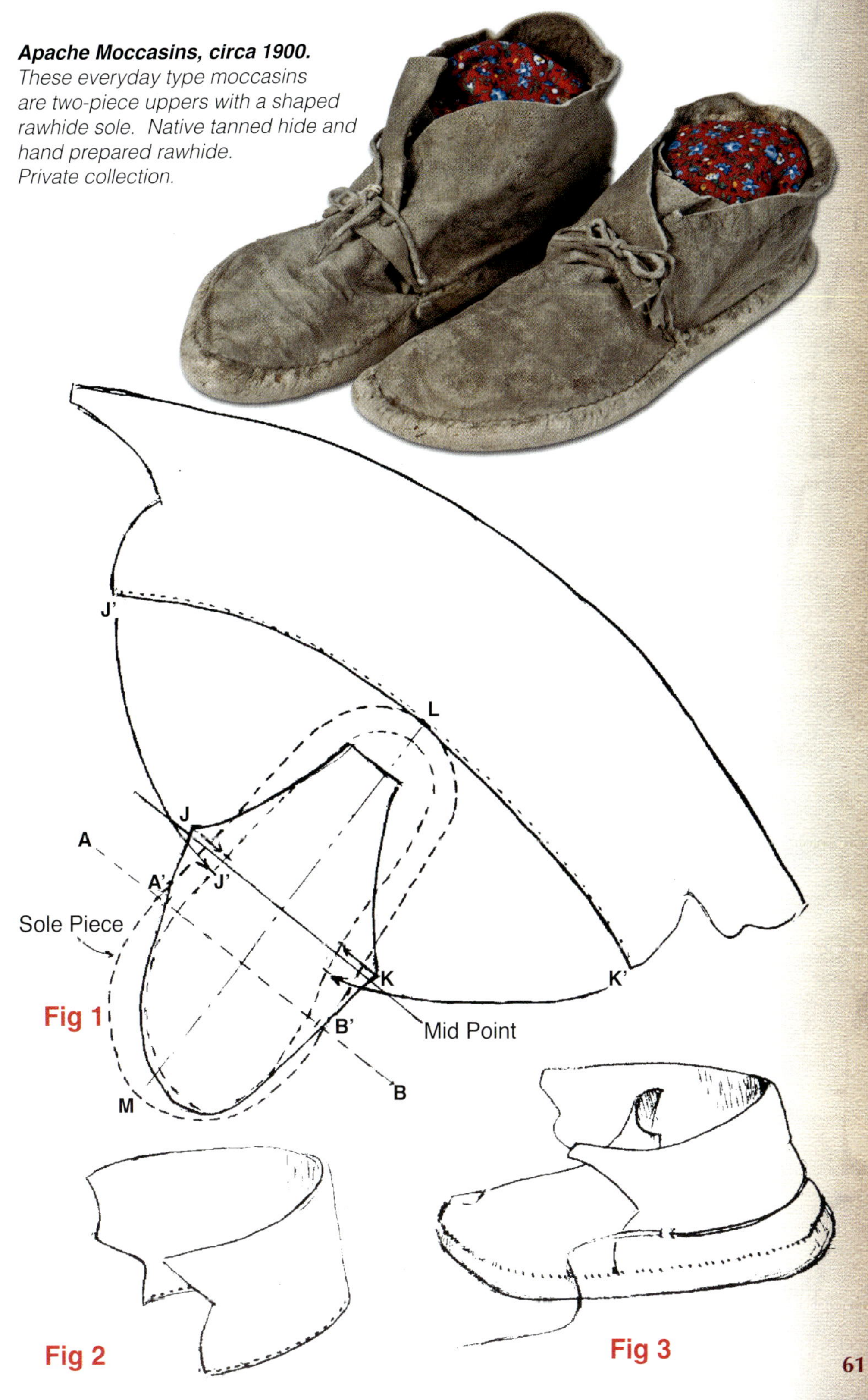

Apache Moccasins, circa 1900.
These everyday type moccasins are two-piece uppers with a shaped rawhide sole. Native tanned hide and hand prepared rawhide.
Private collection.

Apache

Pointed Toe - Two Piece

1. See General Instructions.
2. A B = circumference of foot.
3. A' B' - width of sole piece.
4. L M' = length of sole piece.
5. Sole piece is shown as outer dotted line **L** to **A'** and **M'** and **M'** to **B'** to **L**.
6. Sole width is determined by measuring under the foot on line **A B** and upon the side of foot about 1/2" above floor line.
7. Sole length Is measured on line **L M'**: from heel to big toe, add same at heel as at side and add at toe, 1/4 the length of foot length.
8. In drawing sole around foot tracing notice the pointed toe position in relation to **L M** center line.
9. Fig. 1 shows the upper piece in respect to foot tracing and sole outline. **Fig. 3** shows the upper in more detail. Note the wedge shape insert which is where the tongue **Fig. 2** is sewn. **Caution**: DO NOT make this cut till sole and upper has been sewn. Then cut from **L** to **Y** can be made. The wedge cut is made to adjust the vamp over instep for proper fit. **Fig. 3**
10. The upper piece is sewn from toe point to **X'** or **X** with **X** an **X'** meeting at point **L** of the sole.
11. The point of the sole must be drawn to the point of the upper. This is done by using a 1/8" stitch on the upper and 1/4" stitch on the sole piece, until point **X** or **X'** falls on "**L**" line at heel.
12. After sewing from toe to heel and sewing from **L** to **X X'**, cut the foot opening to fit the arch of foot.
13. The tongue-insert gore can be sewn in to fill the wedge shape below point **Y**
14. The tie string, about 14-18" long, is attached on both sides, (See **Fig. 4**) and through hole in tongue. (See Tongue Detail sheet, page 25.)
15. For added decoration a 2" to 3" wide welt strip can be sewn in heel seam and fringes cut.

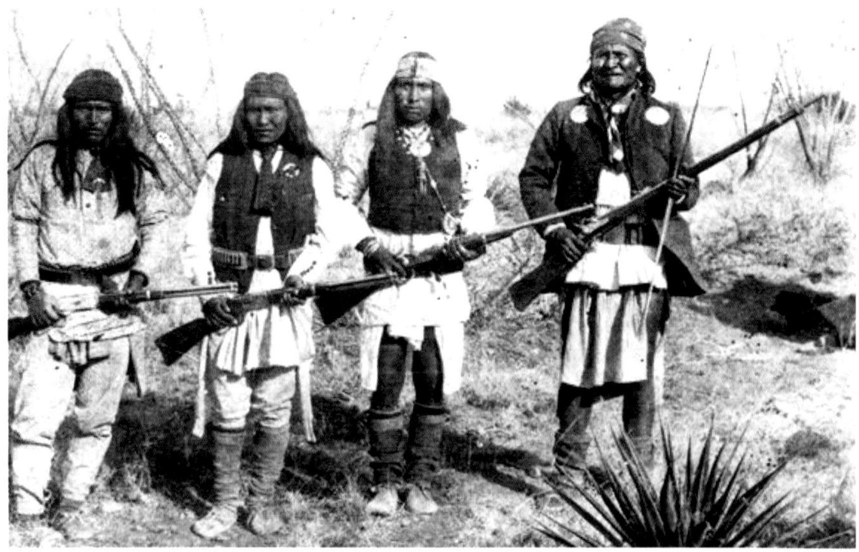

Geronimo and his son, with two warriors - Apache

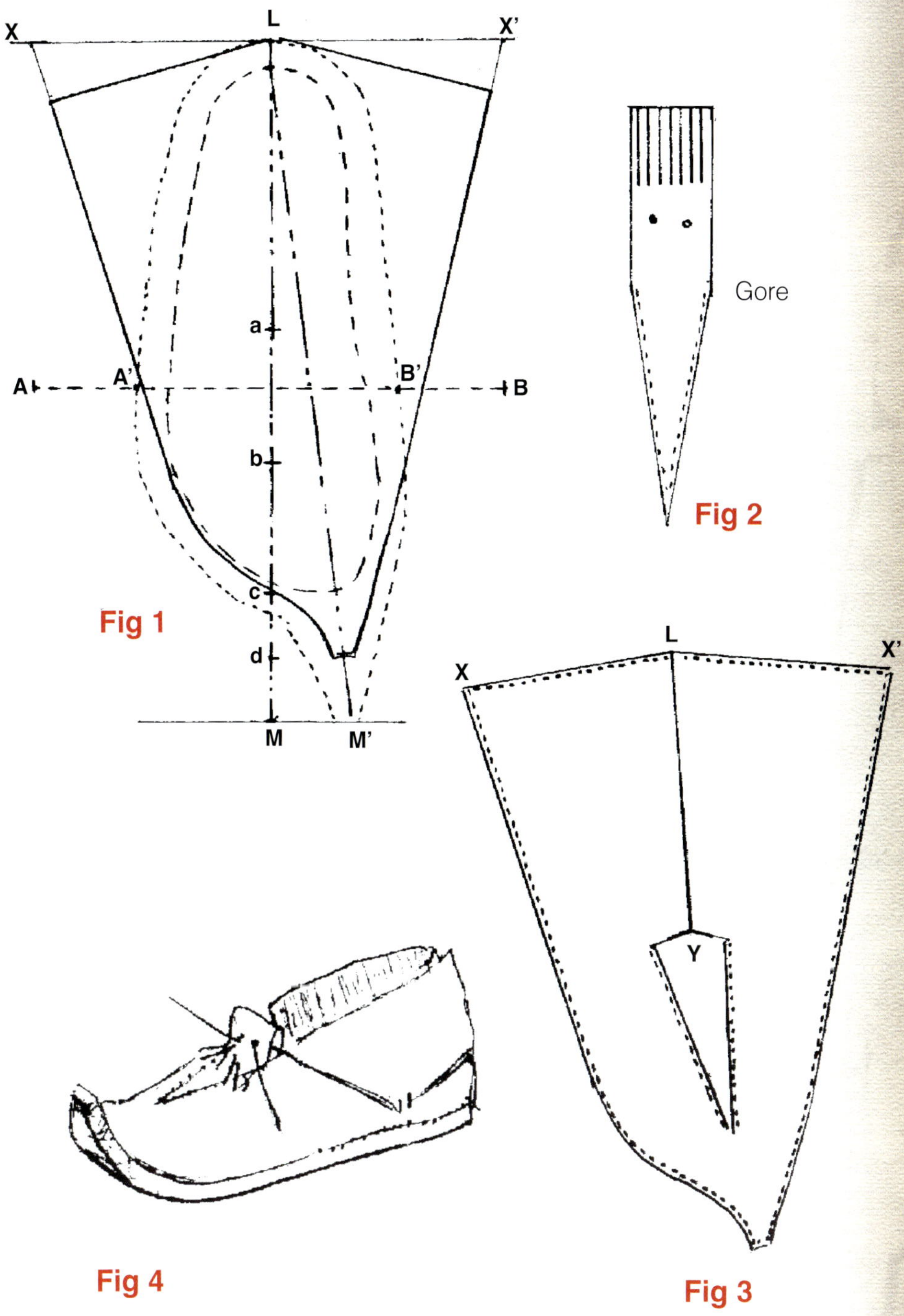

Fig 1

Fig 2

Fig 3

Fig 4

Apache

Pointed Toe - 2-Piece

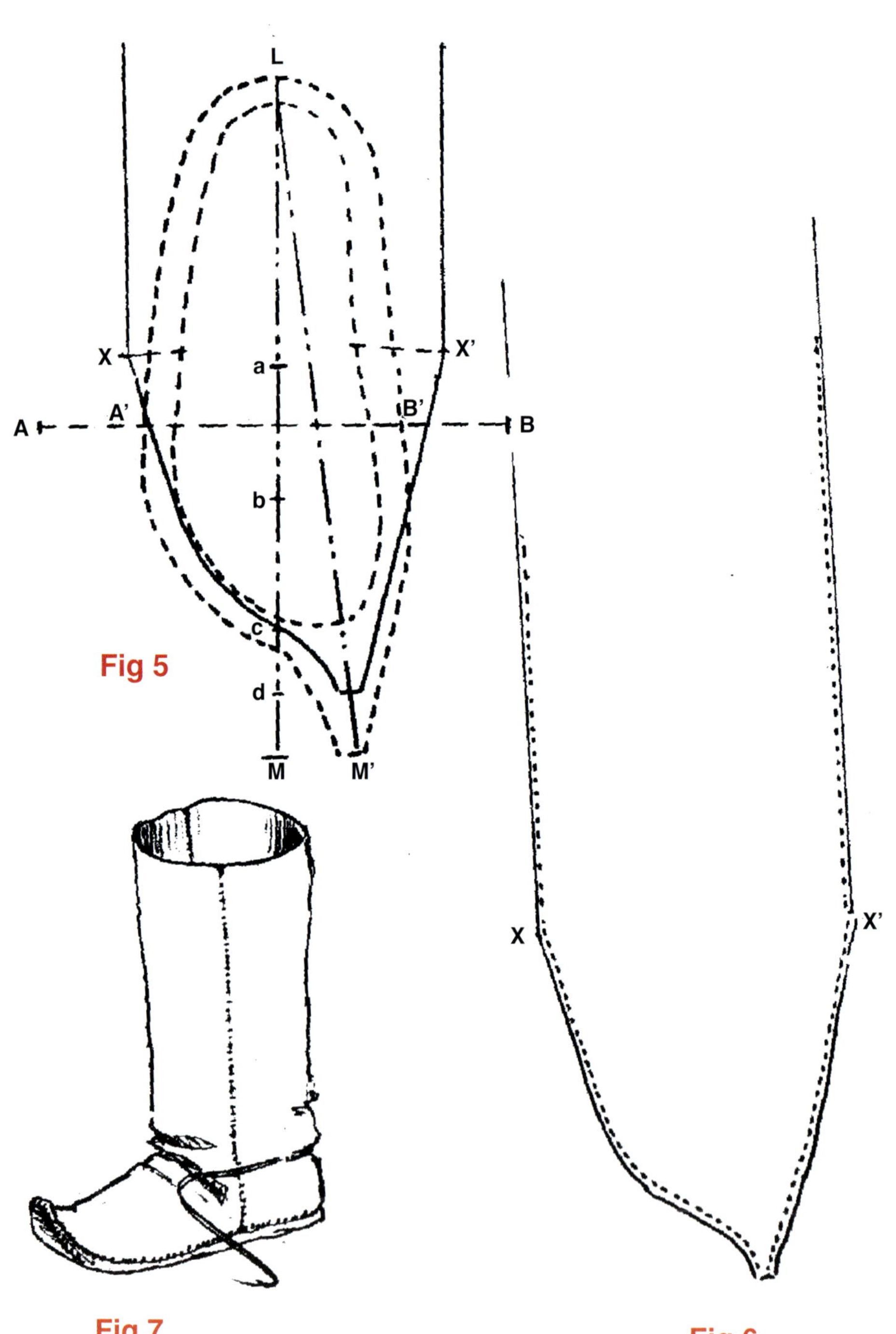

Fig 5

Fig 7

Fig 6

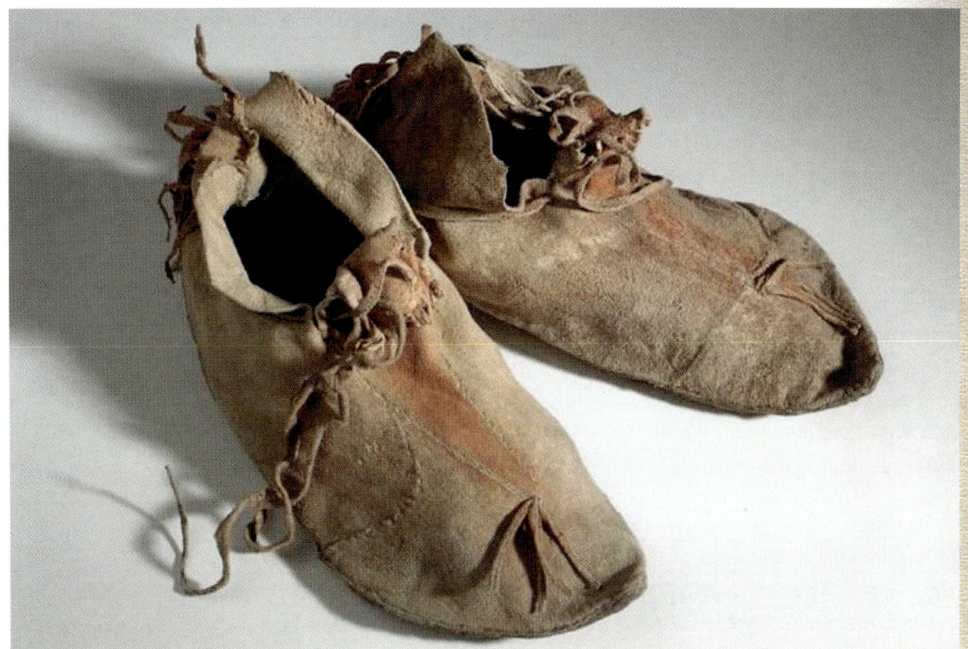

Jicarilla Apache Moccasins, circa 1890. *Featuring only minimal painted decoration, these moccasins illustrate the unique Apache characteristic of placing a "gore" (triangular shaped insert) in the vamp, with the seams often being covered with lanes of beadwork. Courtesy of the Division of Anthropology, American Museum of Natural History, Catalog No. 50_8322AB.*

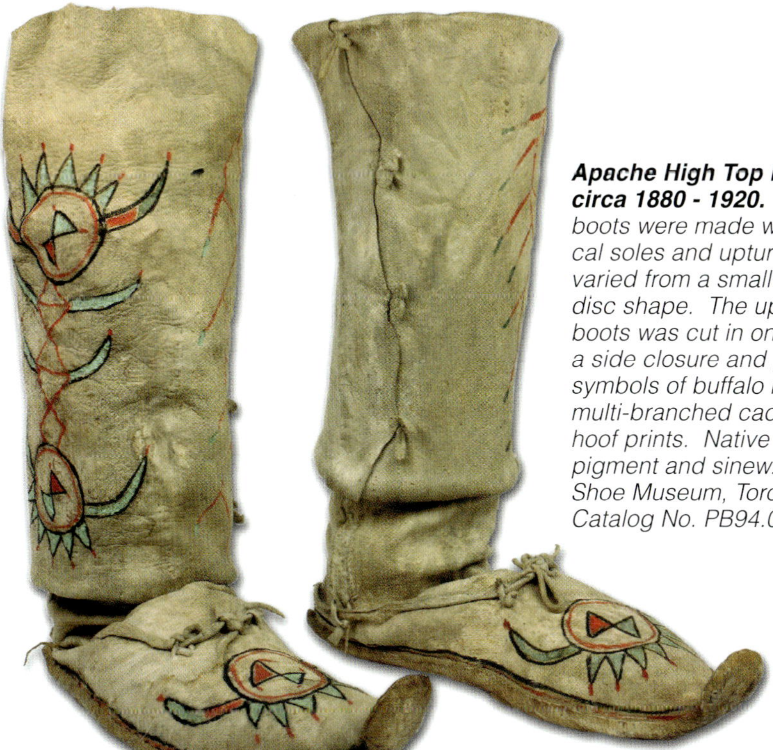

Apache High Top Moccasins, circa 1880 - 1920. *Most Apache boots were made with asymmetrical soles and upturned toes, which varied from a small point to a large disc shape. The upper on these boots was cut in one piece with a side closure and painted with symbols of buffalo head shields, multi-branched cacti, and buffalo hoof prints. Native tanned hide, pigment and sinew. Image © Bata Shoe Museum, Toronto Canada. Catalog No. PB94.0071.*

Northern Plains

Soft Sole, Side-Seam

Historical Background

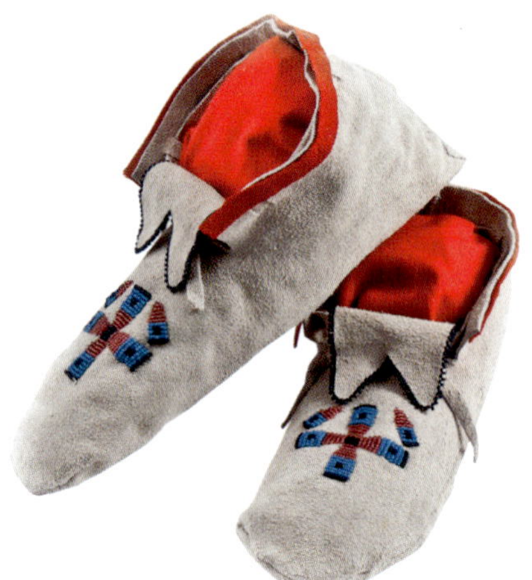

This style of soft-sole, side-seam moccasin was worn up until the 1870's or 1880's by many different Northern Plains tribes throughout U.S. and Canada, including the Blackfeet, Crow, Assiniboine, Cree, Nez Perce, Sarsi, Gros Ventre, Salish, Shoshoni, Mandan, and Hidatsa. It is the forerunner of the hard-sole moccasin and is excellent for use with an early style Indian outfit or with fur trapper or early explorer gear, being simple to make, very practical, and quite comfortable to wear.

1. Begin by drawing a pattern on a large piece of paper. Place your foot on the paper and have someone draw an outline by holding a pencil perpendicular to the floor. Add 1/2" all around, and then draw in a lengthwise center-line.

2. Continue developing the pattern as shown in **Fig. 1**. The shaded area is the original pattern including the 1/2" you added. Mark heel slits 1/2" from the center line (1-1/2" apart). The length of the distance **"W"** is half of your instep circumference, which is found by wrapping a string around your foot and across the arch where a shoestring would be tied. Fold this string in half to get **"W"**. The center line is at a slight angle (25° - 30°) to line **AB**.

3. Make the pattern in **Fig. 2** by cutting out the pattern in **Fig. 1**. Do NOT cut the paper to the left of **AB** at this time, and Do NOT cut along line **AB**. Cut only from **A** around **C** to **B**. fold the paper at **AB**, trace its outline, and transfer points for the original center line to the top and bottom of the new part of the pattern. Cut a "T" shape in the left side of the pattern. As shown in **Fig. 2**. The length of the "T" is 1/2 the length of the center line, **A B**. Now cut out the rest of the pattern.

4. Before transferring the pattern to the leather, it should be pre-stretched in both directions. Cowhide will stretch very little, but buckskin and elk will stretch quite a lot and your moccasins will soon be too big if you do not stretch it before proceeding. Now you can transfer the entire pattern to the leather pieces. We recommend using a pencil or tailors chalk as ink is permanent and will detract from the finished moccasins.

5. Fold the leather at **A B** so it is inside-out from the way you want the finished moccasin. Normally, this would be worn with the suede side out. Cut a 3 foot piece of simulated sinew, split it in half, and make it round by rolling it on your pants leg with the palm of your hand. Using a whip stitch, as shown in **Fig. 3**, sew from **A** around to where **C** and **D** meet. Open the moccasin up and sew the two sides together to form the back seam. Turn the moccasin right side out, fold up the heel tab, and sew as shown in **Fig. 3**.

6. Cut two tongues in the shape shown in **Fig. 4**. Cut two laces from the two remaining leather pieces. Whip-stitch the tongues to the moccasins, cut slits for the lacing as illustrated in **Fig. 3**, and insert the laces.

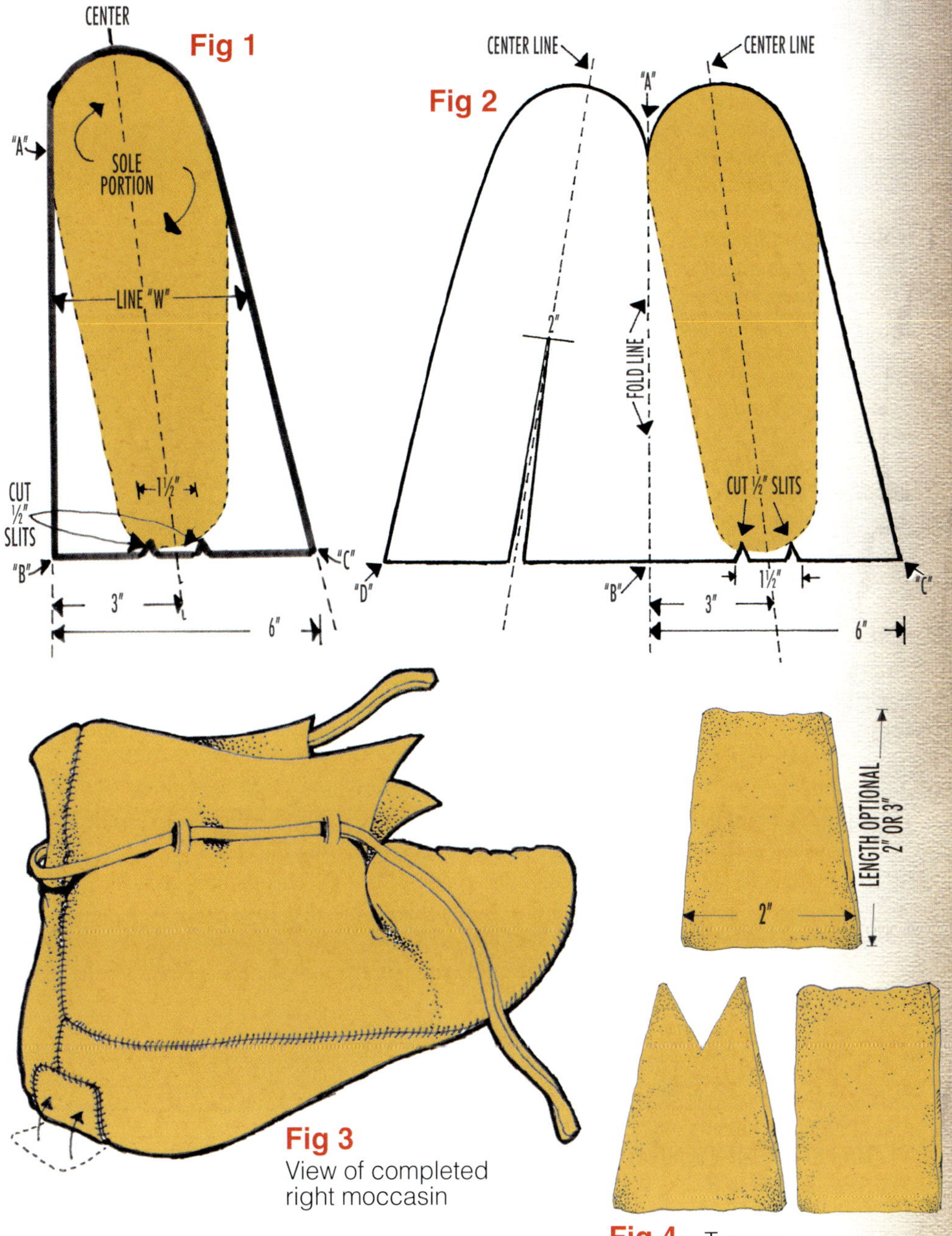

Fig 3 View of completed right moccasin

Fig 4 Tongues

Decoration

This style of moccasin was often either left plain or very simply decorated. Common decorations include a small beaded or quilled "Maltese" cross, keyhole type rosette, or Blackfoot style "U" on the vamp. Additional decorations may include binding the top edge of the cuffs with wool or calico cloth and edge beading around the tongue. For more ideas, we recommend studying actual museum examples or photos in museum catalogs, as well as old photographs from your particular tribal style.

Plateau

Kootenai

Center Seam

The Kootenai people originally lived along the Kootenai River in Idaho, Montana and British Columbia. They were hunter-gatherers, and salmon was an important staple to their diets. They had permanent winter villages of cone-shaped houses made from wooden poles and rush mats. In 1855, the tribe signed a treaty with the US government, and the Dawes Act broke up tribal land holdings into individual allotments. Since 1986, the Kootenai Tribe has owned and operated the Kootenai River Inn Casino and Spa and other operations located in Bonners Ferry, Idaho. Reservation industries include timber, tourism, and selling sand and gravel, and the tribe also owns a sturgeon hatchery.

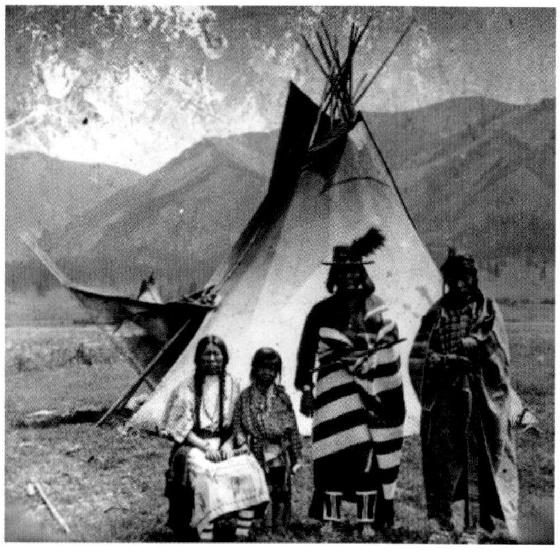

Kootenai (Flathead) family camp in Idaho, circa 1890.

1. See **Fig. 1** for general design.
2. **A B** line is the circumference line and must include the tongue insert and the sole piece. (Note change in position of line **A' B'**.)
3. The length of the sole piece can be determined by measuring **L M** line; allow 3/4" at heel and measure under big toe and over to base of big toe nail. (See **Fig. G-3A,** page 21.)
4. Determine curve at **M** by dividing width in three parts. (See **Fig. 1**.)
5. The depth is found on line **L M** and intersection of line **C**. This point is on **L M**. (3/4" at heel + length of foot tracing + 1/2" at toe.) This also gives point **A'** which is midway between **X** and **C**.
6. **H K** and **H' K'** are set at a 100 degree angle for average foot; increase angle for broad foot or decrease angle for narrow foot.
7. Length of **H K** is about 1/3 or length **A B**.
8. Cut out pattern. (Fold paper on line **L M**, so both sides will be symmetrical.)
9. See General Instructions, Steps 12-15.
10. Fold leather inside out.
11. Bring **H** and **H'** together. Use whipstitch with 1/8" spacing. (See **Fig. 2**)
12. Sew from **H** to **K**.
13. Gather toe flap (center point) to **K** and **K'**.
14. Use 1/8" spacing on **K** side, but use 1/4" spacing of curve of flap as it must be "gathered" to the **K** side. Tie off all thread and endings.
15. Return to **K'** and repeat spacing to complete toe.
16. Cut out "tongue insert". Place it on moccasin at the center point of **H H'**. (See **Fig. 2**.)
17. Repeat spacing of 1/8" on tongue insert and 1/4" spacing on side pieces as they must be gathered.
18. Sew both sides the same till the "foot opening" equals 1/2 the length of the moccasin.
19. Bring heel point **X X'** together and sew down the heel cut. (See page 24)
20. Turn moccasin right side-out. Notch the heel tab.

21. Extensions can be added around foot opening if desired. This piece will be foot length plus 4 inches; the height can vary, but a “wrap around top” will be 5 to 6 inches in width.
22. Sew extensions by allowing 2” flap at the tongue seam. (See **Fig. G-9**, page 23)
23. Tie string is attached at 4 to 6 places around the moccasin. (See **Fig. 3**) All tie holes are made by a round awl such as an ice pick. They are never cut.
24. Length of tie strings are about 36” for a “wrap-around top”.
25. Strings are made from scrap. (See **G-11**, page 23.)

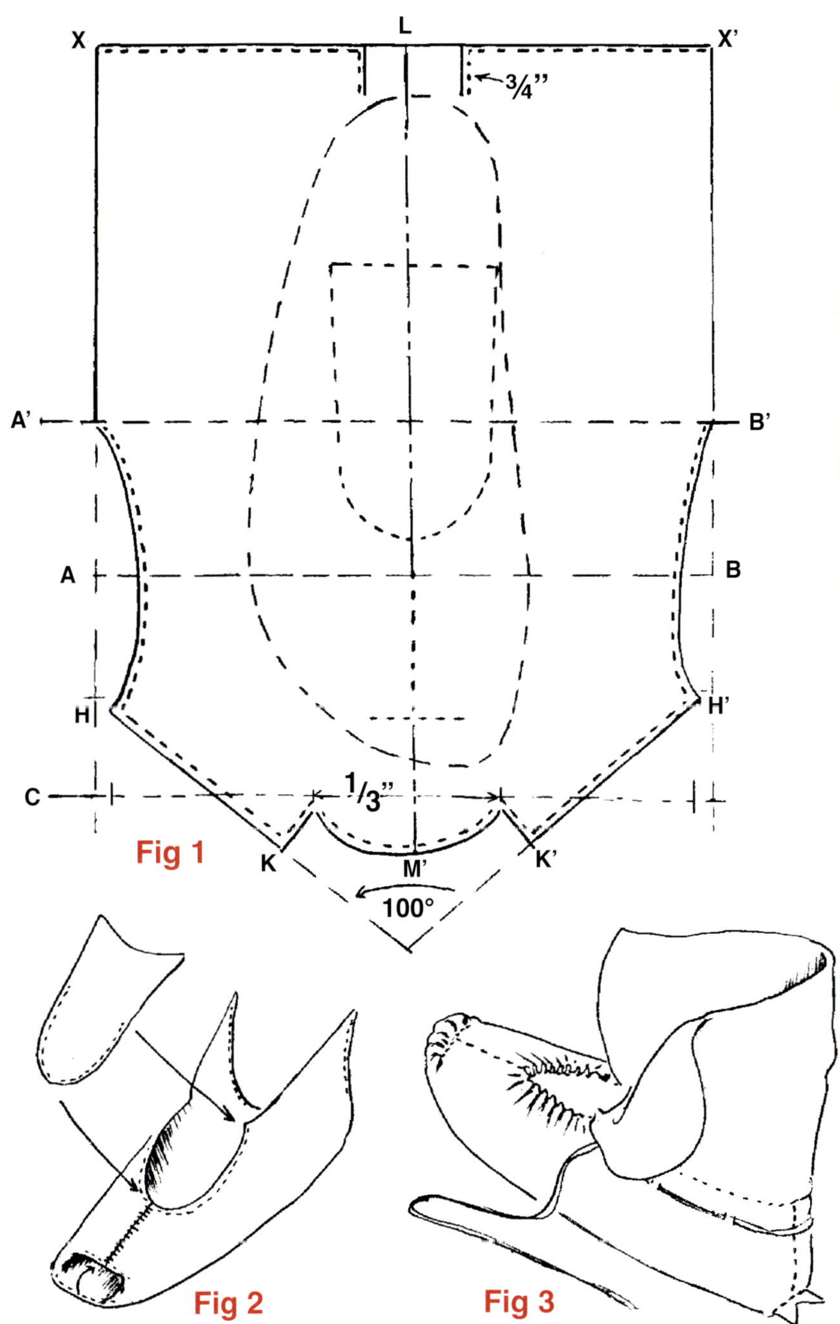

Fig 1

Fig 2

Fig 3

Salish (Flathead)

Side Seam

The Salish, meaning "the people", were called Flathead Indians by Europeans who came to the area, although they never practiced head flattening. Originally, they lived east of the Continental Divide, with headquarters near the eastern slope of the Rocky Mountains. Later, they ventured west, living in the Pacific Northwest, between the Cascade Mountains and Rocky Mountains. Today, the Confederated Salish and Kootenai Tribes of the Flathead Reservation are the Bitterroot Salish, Kootenai and Pend d'Oreilles (pronounced: "pond-oray") tribes, with members living both on and off the reservation.

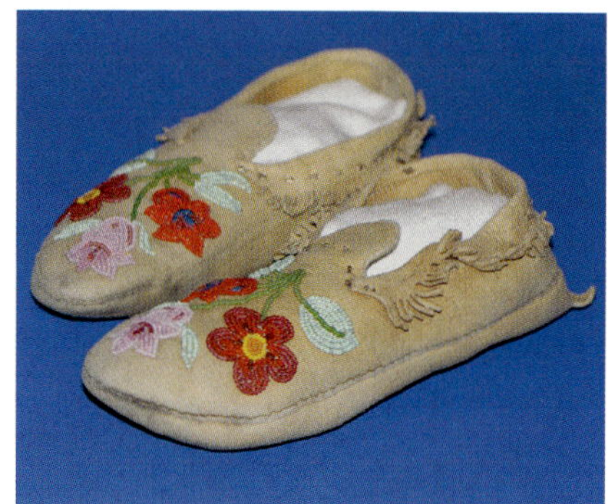

Salish Side Seam Moccasins, circa 1900. *Smoked, brain tanned buckskin with floral applique beadwork. note the use of a welt in the seam. Joe Rosenthal collection.*

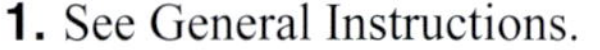

1. See General Instructions.
2. Make foot tracing.
3. Measure **A B** (allow 1/4" for seam) See **Fig. 1**.
4. Fold paper on line **L M** so that **A** and **B** come together, and foot tracing is located as shown in **Fig. 1**.
5. Allow about 3/4" at heel and 1/2" at toe at line **L M**. (This measurement is for average foot of 9" to 12" long and medium weight leather.)
6. Cut folded paper from **L** through points **M** to **M'**.
7. This pattern is for either left or right foot.
8. Trace pattern of leather. (See General Instructions.)
9. Cut leather.
10. Foot tracing can be cut now or later. **<u>Caution</u>**: Be sure to cut opening so that there is a left and right moccasin, and that grain or flesh sides of leather are matched.
11. The foot opening **L'** to **J K** line (See **Fig. 1**) is 1/2 the length of **L M**. **J K** is about 2" long.
12. Note dotted tongue position is wider than **J K**. This gives a tuck-in tip as shown in Tongue Detail sheet on page 25.
13. The tongue, **Fig. 2**, can be made of scrap or flank leather, about 2 1/2" wide and 6 to 8 " long.
14. Fold both pieces of leather grain side in. Start sewing at **M'** and around to **X X'**. Be sure to check points **X** and **X'** occasionally during sewing to see that they match. Some sewing produces a "creeping" of the leather and as a result the points **X** and **X'** do not end up even.
15. Tie off thread at point **X X'** and if foot opening has been cut, start at **L'** and sew to within 3/4" of bottom. See Heel Detail sheet, page 24.
16. Sew heel and tab before turning inside out.
17. Sew on tongue. Lay tongue grain side down on vamp and bring edge to line **J K** and sew. See Tongue Detail, page 25.
18. The tops or extensions are usually 6" wide or higher and are 5" to 6" longer than the length of **L M** or length of moccasin.
19. Note **Fig. G-9,** page 23. The long side of top flap fold over the other short side from the inside to outside.
20. Lay top piece against the foot opening (See **Fig. G-9**) grain side down.
21. Tie both ends of this seam securely.
22. Tie strings can be attached next. See Tongue Detail **U**, page 24.
23. Make strings at least 36" long. See **Fig. G-11**, page 23.

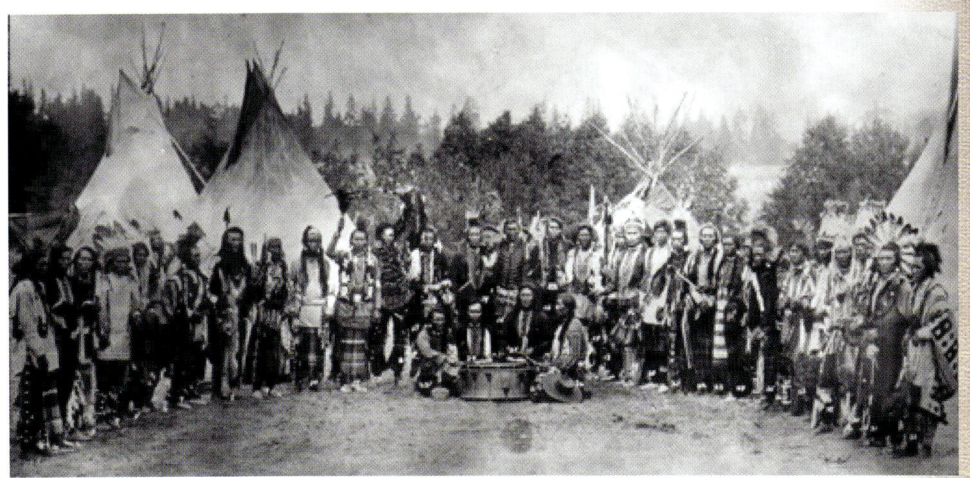

Salish men on July 4th, 1903 standing by tepees near St. Ignatius Mission, Flathead Reservation, Montana.

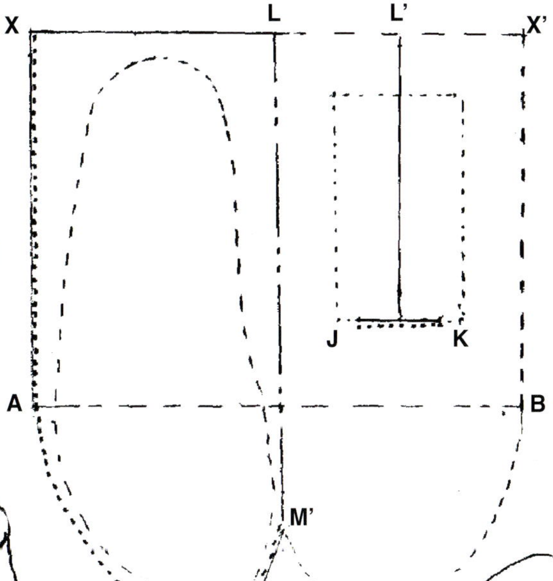

X L L' X'

Fig 1

J K

Fig 2

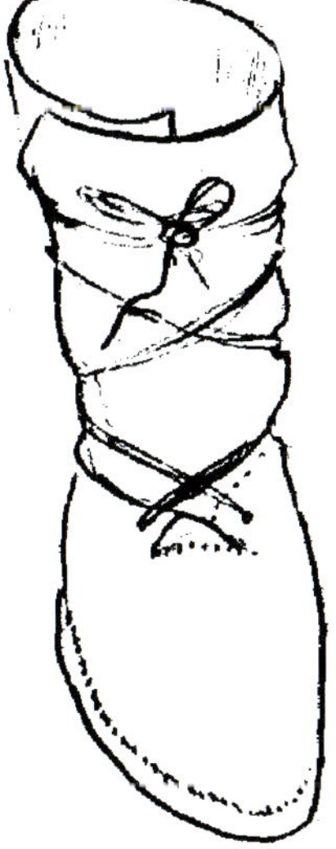

A B

M'

M

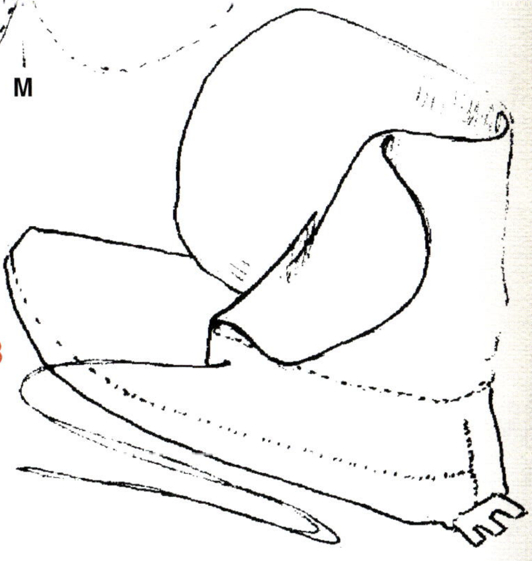

Fig 3

Fig 4

Salish - Tongue Variations

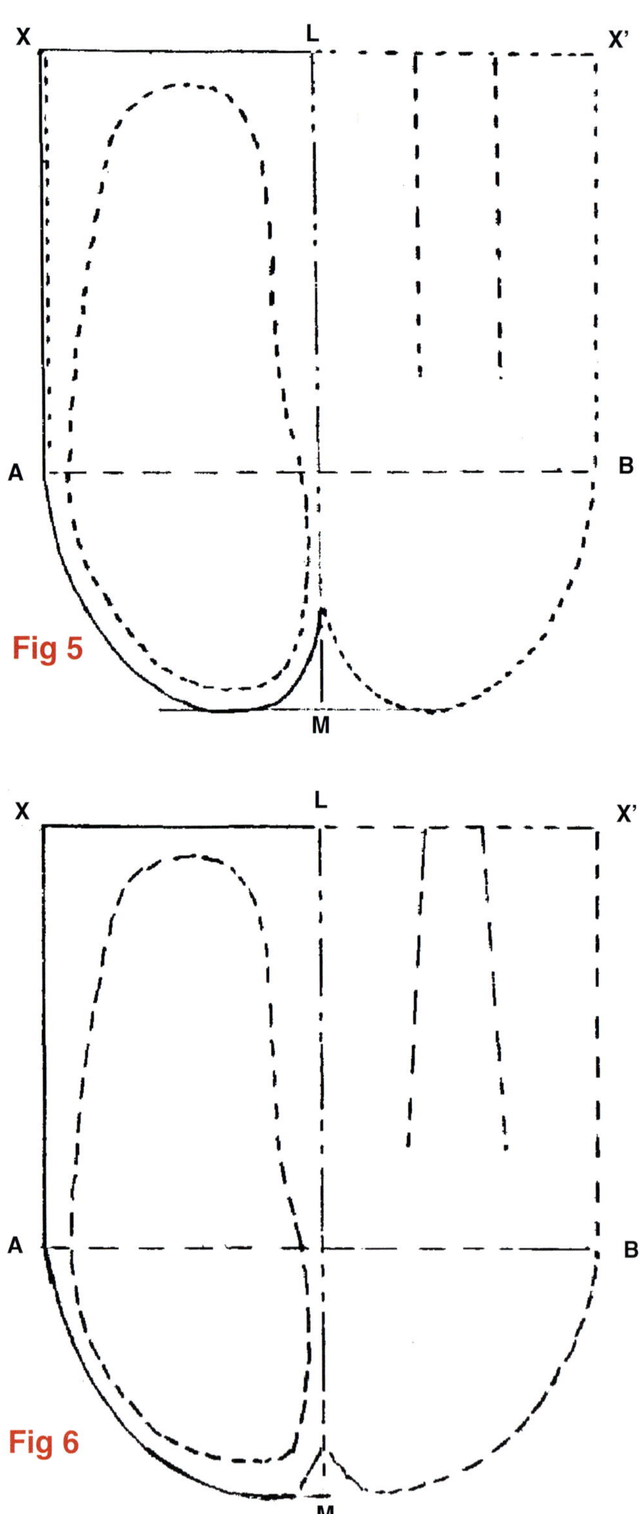

UTE

Hard Sole Type

Ute people are indigenous to the Great Basin and are now living primarily on three tribal reservations in Utah and Colorado. The Utes were established in the Four Corners area by 1500 A.D. and were hunters and gatherers who moved on foot to hunting grounds and gathering land based upon the season. In the western part of their territory, the Utes lived in wickiups and ramadas; Hide tipis were used in the eastern reaches of their territory. Unlike many other tribal groups in this region, the Utes have no tradition or evidence of historic migration to the areas now known as Colorado and Utah, and ancestors of the Ute appear to have occupied this area or nearby areas for at least a thousand years.

1. See General Instructions.
2. Note in particular - conditions along line **A B**. The dotted foot outline and points **A' B'** of the vamp-upper piece are more than circumference of **A B**. This makes the moccasin a bit loose over arch. This is desirable with a hard sole.
3. Note also **X** and **X'** are dropped down form the horizontal line. This is because the distance from **A'** to **L** must equal distance from **A'** to **X**.
4. The tongue can be cut before sewing, cut from **L** to **J** and **L** to **K**. Distance between **J** and **K** will be about 2".
5. This particular tongue design is often found in baby moccasins, as there is no harsh seam to bite into the baby's foot.
6. The sole, if hard sole, will be about 1/4" longer than foot outline.
7. Sew from **M** to heel. Take a bit wider stitch in vamp piece than sole and the vamp a greater distance around the toe.
8. Sew up on heel seam. Start at the sole seam and if the leather varies and ends up uneven at the top; it can be trimmed.
9. The tie string is about 16" long.
10. Tops may be added if desired. (See **Fig. G-10**, page 23).

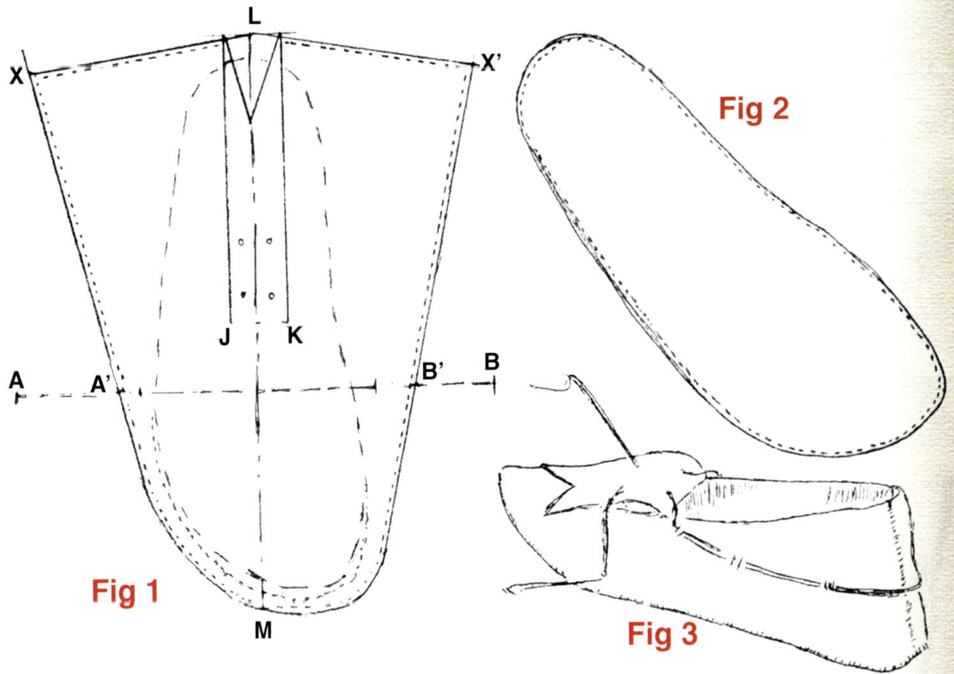

Southwest

Navajo & Pueblo

The Navajo, or Diné, of the Southwestern U.S. are believed to have migrated from northwestern Canada and eastern Alaska where the majority of other Athapascan speakers reside. Up until the 1800s, the Navajo were largely hunters, gatherers and raiders. Contact with the Spanish in the mid-1500s, as well as the Pueblo people, introduced them to sheep and crop farming, and silver workingi techniques, although they continued hunting and raiding. By the early 1700s, they began some weaving of blankets and garments, a skill they learned from the Pueblo people. By the late 1800s, they were overcome by the U.S. military and sent to reservations, where they were forced completely to adapt to farming and sheep herding. Today, the majority of Navajos continue to live on their traditional lands in New Mexico and Arizona.

1. See General Instructions.
2. A B = circumference of foot.
3. A' B' = width of sole leather.
4. L M = length of sole piece.
5. A' B' and **L M** measurements should be 3/4" to 1" above floor line.
6. Two sole pieces will be made: one for the right foot and one for the left. Cut from similar leather.
7. Two vamp-tops are cut for left and right. See **Fig. 1** - solid line.
8. The sole pieces are moistened to aid in shaping. A draw string can be used as with the other "shaped soles". (See **Fig. 2** on page 85 and **Fig. 1** on page 17).
9. C' (on both foot outlines) marks end of sewing from **M** to **C'**. **C'** to **C** is sewn later as sewing is completed, from **M D** and **D X** around the sole. **X** is joined to point **C'** under **Y** flap.
10. Sewing is done outside out and can be done in the usual manner or laced by prepunching the hole in sole and vamp pieces. This method requires considerable attention to spacing of holes as the sole must be "gathered".

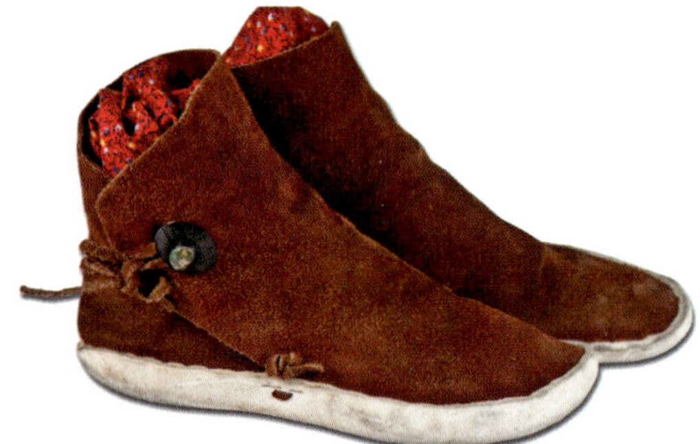

Navajo or Pueblo Boot Moccasins. *Typical style moccasins with a soft leather upper and heavy leather "shaped" sole. The uppers have been dyed brown. Private Collection.*

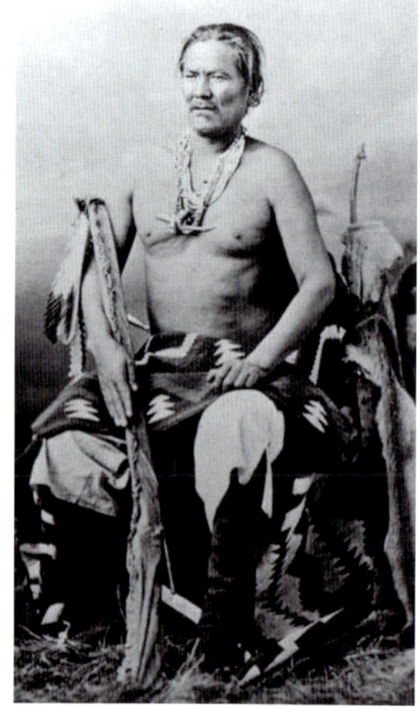

"Studio portrait of Manuelito, once fierce chief of the Navajo, taken between 1887 and 1901. He holds a rifle in a buckskin scabbard and wears moccasin boots, a blanket, and bead necklaces with a saber pendant. Western History/Genealogy Department, Denver Public Library"

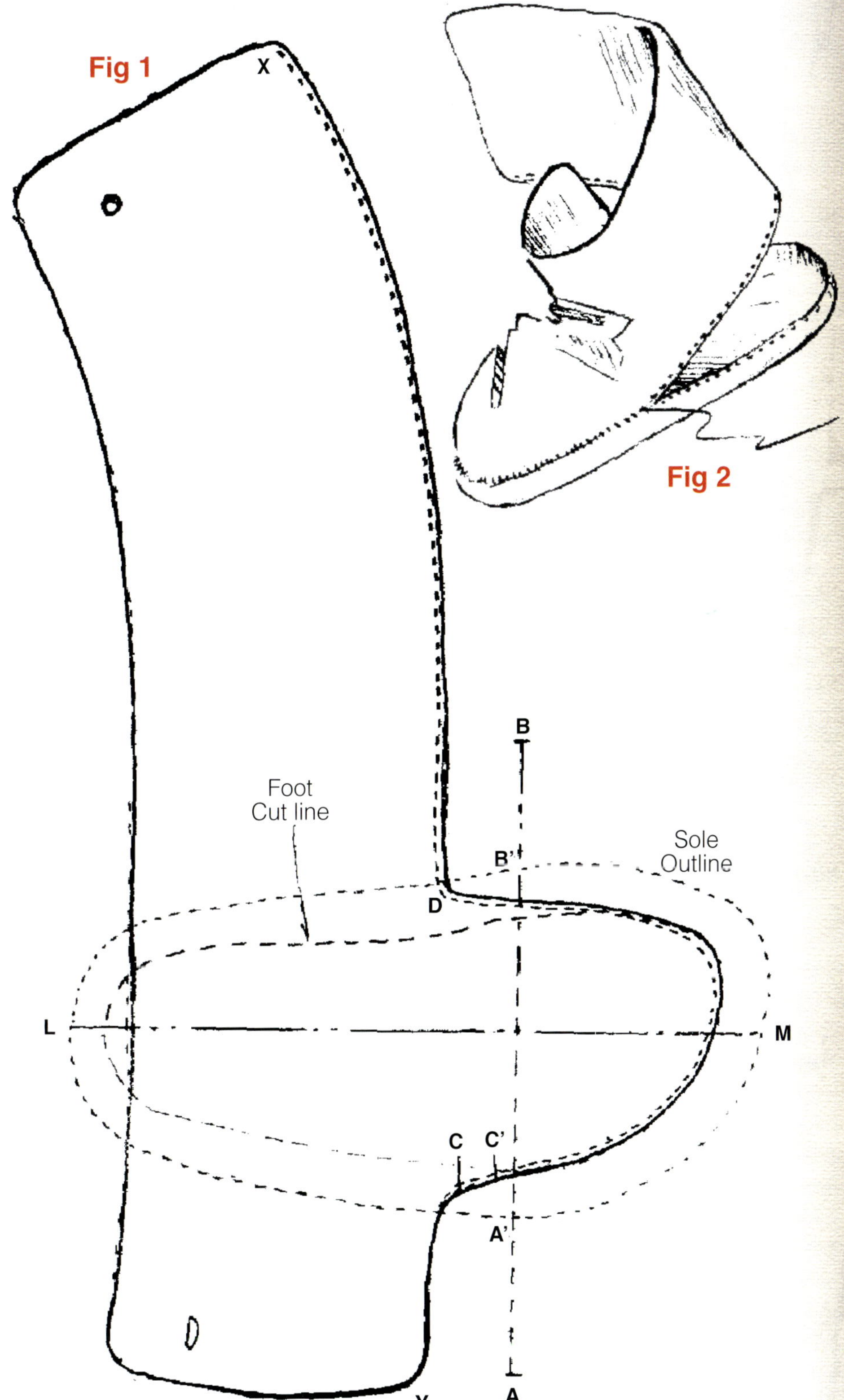
Fig 1
X
Fig 2
B
Foot
Cut line
Sole
Outline
B'
D
L
M
C
C'
A'
Y
A

Paiute

Shaped Sole - Two Piece

The Paiute belong to the Uto-Aztecan family of Native American languages. The Northern Paiute traditionally have lived in the Great Basin in eastern California, western Nevada, and southeast Oregon. Relations among the Northern Paiute bands and their Shoshone neighbors were generally peaceful, and today, they reside in Nevada. The Southern Paiute traditionally lived in the Colorado River Basin and Mohave Desert in northern Arizona and southeastern California and often traded with coastal tribes of the Owens Valley and the central coast. The introduction of European settlers and agricultural practices made it difficult for the Southern Paiute to continue their traditional lifestyle, as it drove away the game and reduced their ability to hunt, as well as to gather natural foods. Today, Southern Paiute communities are located in Utah, Arizona and California.

1. See General Instructions.
2. A B = circumference of foot. (**Fig. 1**)
3. A'B' = width of sole piece which is measured underfoot and upon side of foot about 3/4" above floor line.
4. The vamp or upper piece at line **A B** is wider than usual. Note this on pattern. The tie string is located to draw the foot opening closed.
5. Note the two lines from Point **X** to toes and **X'** to toe. The outside lines will make the back high (if so desired) the inner line will lower the height of the back.
6. Cut two upper pieces, one for each foot.
7. The easiest way to shape the sole is to put a draw string around toes and heel. (See **Fig. 1** on page 17). Draw toe and heel in until sole is size of foot tracing or fits the foot itself.
8. After shaping soles, sew from **M** to heel. Use a whip stitch and tie the "gathers" of the sole to the vamp.
9. Do not make tie string holes until after sewing and putting on foot.
10. This same design can be used with a flat parfleche sole by adjusting measurements.

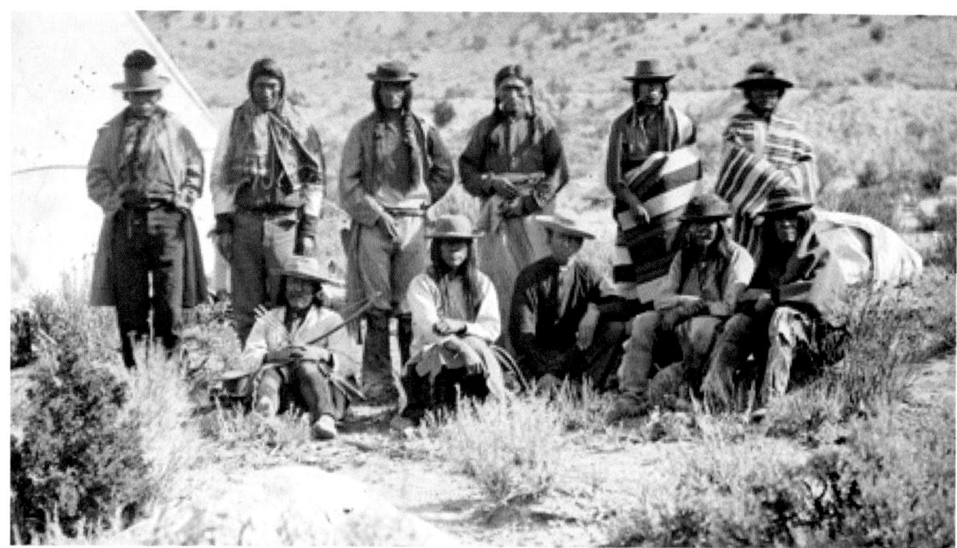

A group of Paiute Indians near Cedar, Utah, in 1872. Photo by Timothy O'Sullivan

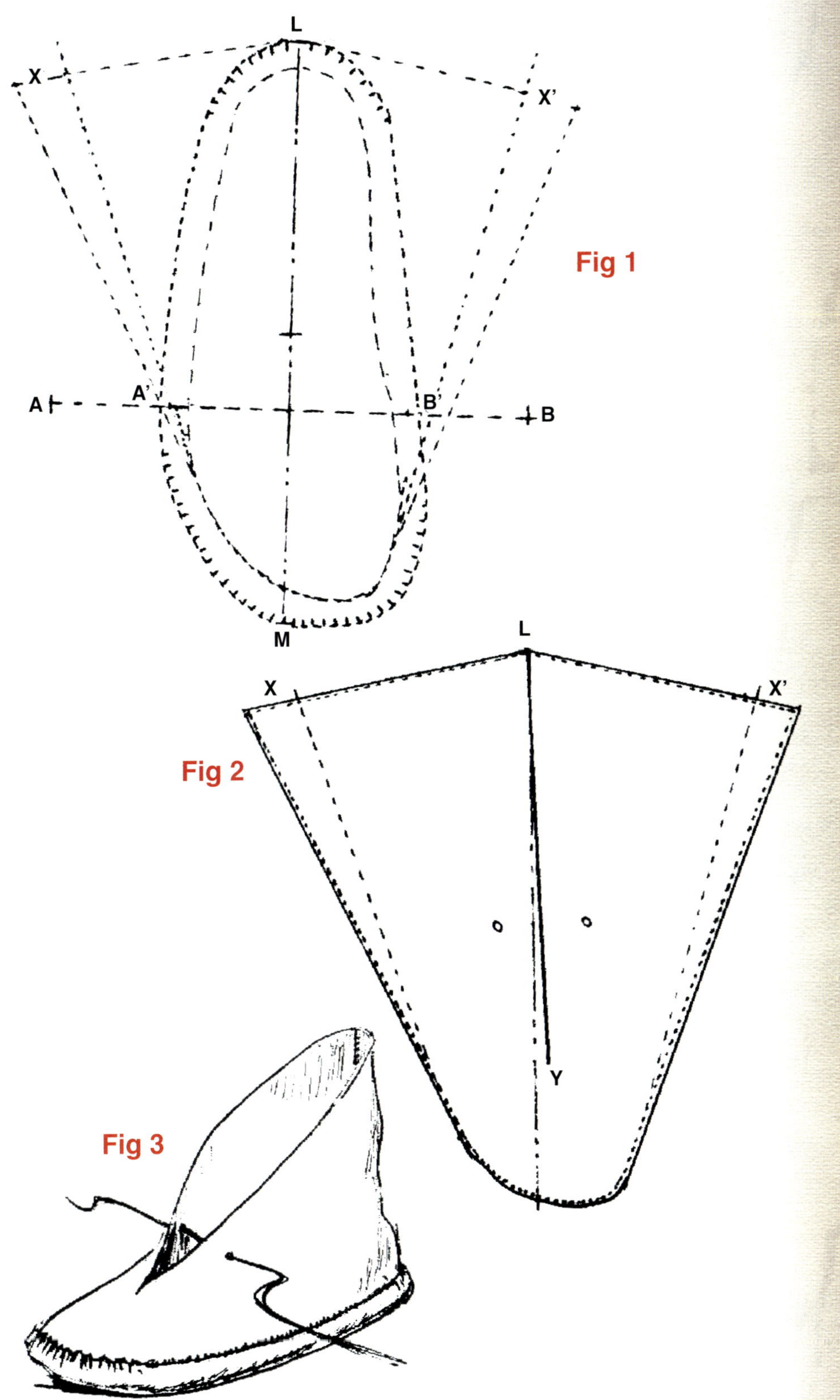
L
X
X'
Fig 1
A
A'
B'
B
M
L
X
X'
Fig 2
Y
Fig 3

Alaska and Canada

Yellow Knives

Center Seam

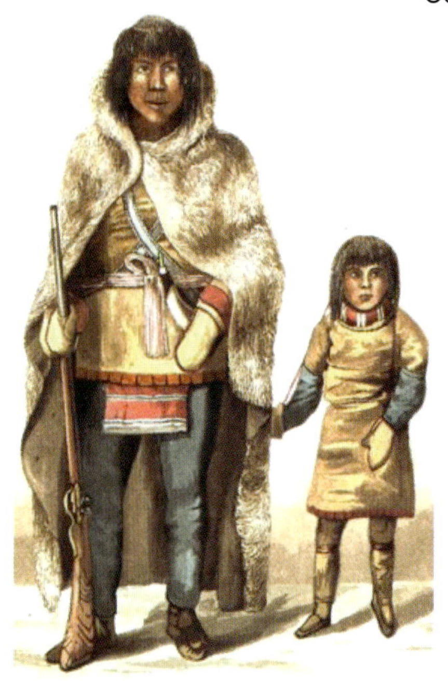

The Yellowknives, Yellow Knives, Copper Indians, Red Knives or Dogrib are Aboriginal peoples of Canada, one of the five main groups of the Dene indigenous people that live in the Northwest Territories of Canada. The name, which is also the source for the later community of Yellowknife, derives from the color of their tools made from copper deposits. The historic Yellowknives lived north and northeast of the Great Slave Lake around the Yellowknife River and Yellowknife Bay and northward along the Coppermine River, northeast to the Black River and east to the Thelon River. Today, these people reside at Fort Resolution, Yellowknife, and other areas of Canada.

Akaitcho, the leader of the Yellowknife Indians, who assisted John Franklin on his expedition to the Coppermine River, with his son, circa 1821.

1. See General Instructions.
2. Special instructions as follows:
3. Line **L M** - (length of foot plus 3/4" at heel plus 1/2" at toe)
4. A B measures circumference.
5. A' B' measures leather which added to tongue insert is equal to **A B** or (**A A'** = 1/2 width of tongue.)
6. O K = 1/2 **H K**
7. Make pattern: trace foot, draw all measurements on pattern.
8. Fold pattern on line **L M** and cut both sides symmetrical.
9. Trace pattern on leather. (See General Instructions for tracing on leather.) Cut two leather patterns alike as there is no right or left.)
10. Fold leather inside out.
11. Sewing: join **H H'** and sew to **K K'**. Use 1/8" stitching.
12. Sew toe with 1/8" stitch and turn right side out.
13. Cut out tongue piece. (See **Fig. 3** for shape.) Width of tongue should be equal to **A B** when added to **A' B'**. Length where stitched to moccasin is about 1/4 length of foot tracing.
14. Center tongue as it appears in **Fig. 1**. Start sewing at **H H'** (see **Fig. 5**) Use 1/8" stitch on the tongue and 1/4" stitch on side piece as sides must be gathered. Sew to **B'** tie off and sew second half of tongue.
15. Sew heel either inside out or right side out. (See Heel Detail on page 24.)
16. Cut out and sew on extensions. (See **Fig. G-9 & G-10** on page 23.)
17. Tie strings and extensions. (See page 68, numbers 23 -25.)

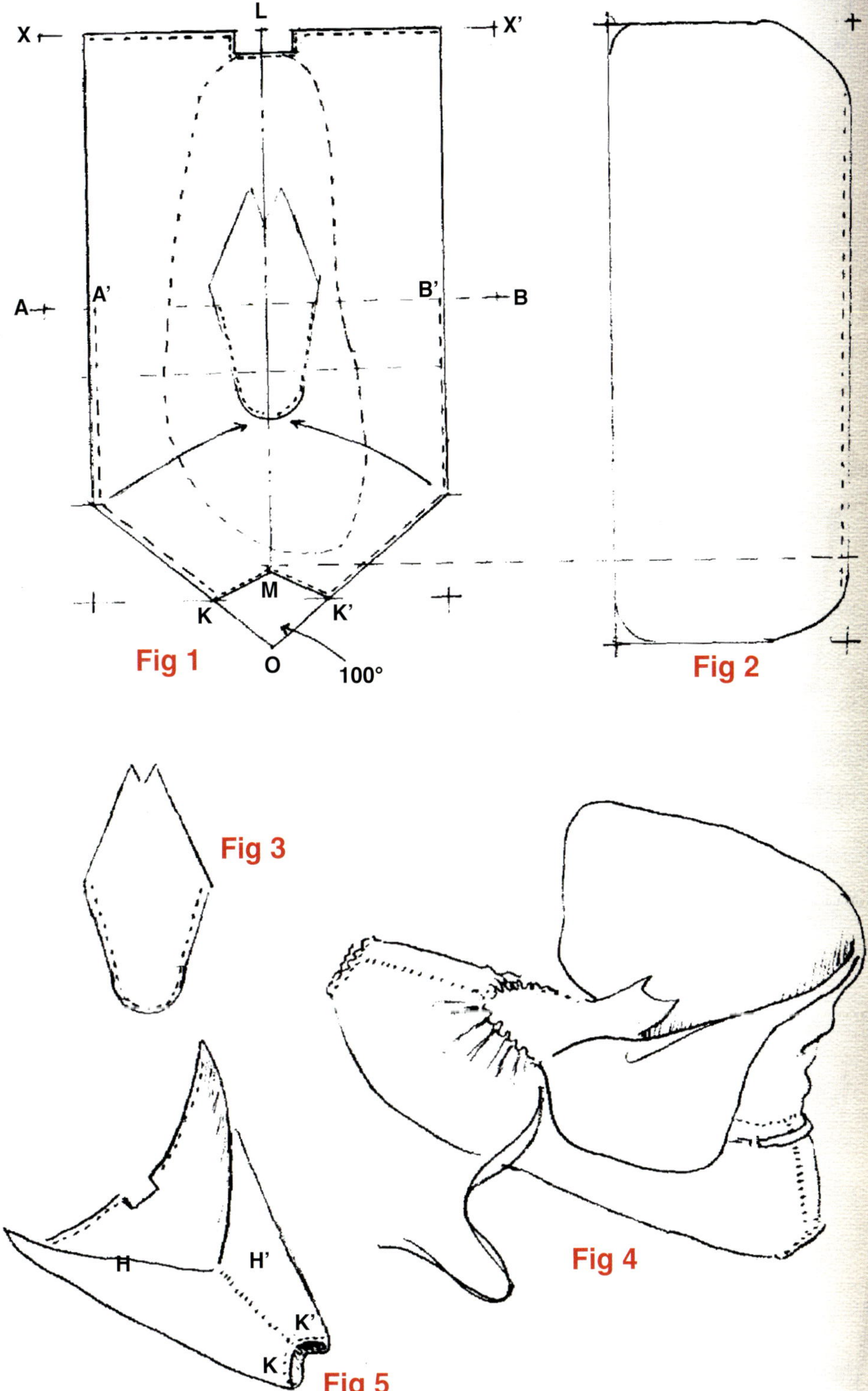
L
X
X'
A
A'
B'
B
M
K
K'
O
100°
Fig 1
Fig 2
Fig 3
Fig 4
H
H'
K'
K
Fig 5

Yukon

Gather Toe (Wrap Around)

1. See general instructions.
2. A B = circumference
3. A' B' plus insert tongue = **A B** (**Fig. 2**).
4. L M is leather length with allowance at heel (1/2" to 3/4") under foot to base of big toe nail. (See **Fig. G-3**, page 21)
4. This moccasin is suited to heavy leather such as moose or elk. Heavy leather usually means wider spacing in stitches.
5. Bring insert **M** to sole **M** and sew to point beyond **A** or **B**. Use wider stitch but keep a 2 to 1 ratio, so as to "gather" the sole piece to the insert.
7. The foot opening is a bit larger for this pattern. (More than 1/2 the length of moccasin).
8. Heel is sewn from **X X'** to **L**.
9. The heel tab is tacked with a few stitches on outside. See Heel Details on page 24.
10. Wrap around tops are most always folded to outside.
11. The length of tops is usually determined by adding 5" to 6" to length of moccasin. Height of tops can be 6" to 8".
12. Sew on tops same as **Fig. G-9**, page 23.
13. Be sure to tie off or bind the beginning and ending stitch on all tops as they receive strain at this point.
14. This pattern has no left or right foot, except by wearing.
15. Note the position of tie strings. Strings are cut (See **Fig. G-11** page 23) from scrap and are about 36" long.
16. Holes for tie-strings are forced open with an awl or pointed tool. They are never cut.

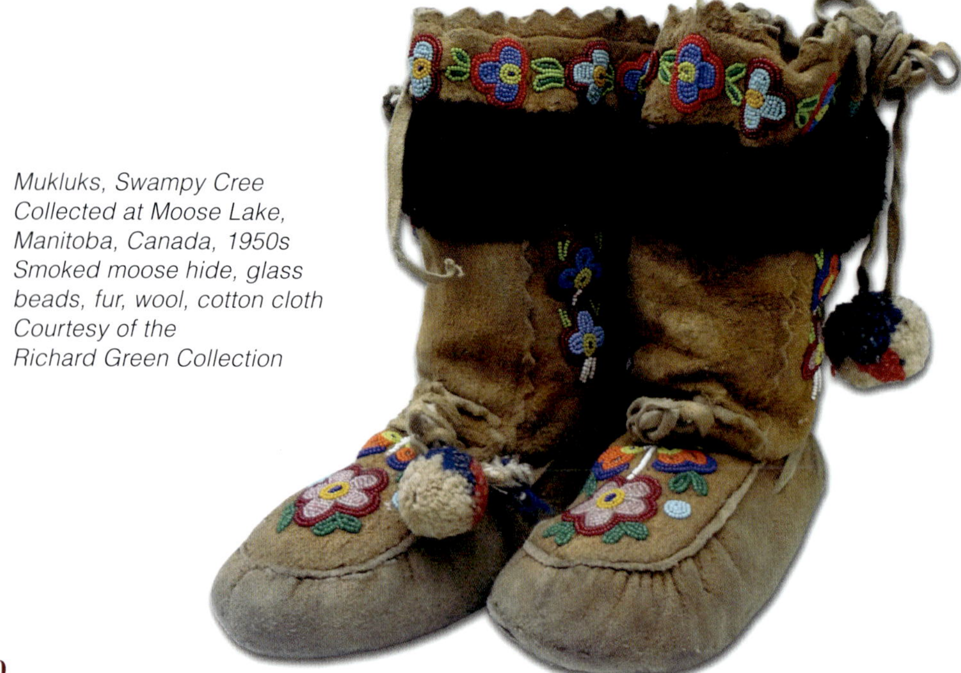

Mukluks, Swampy Cree
Collected at Moose Lake, Manitoba, Canada, 1950s
Smoked moose hide, glass beads, fur, wool, cotton cloth
Courtesy of the Richard Green Collection

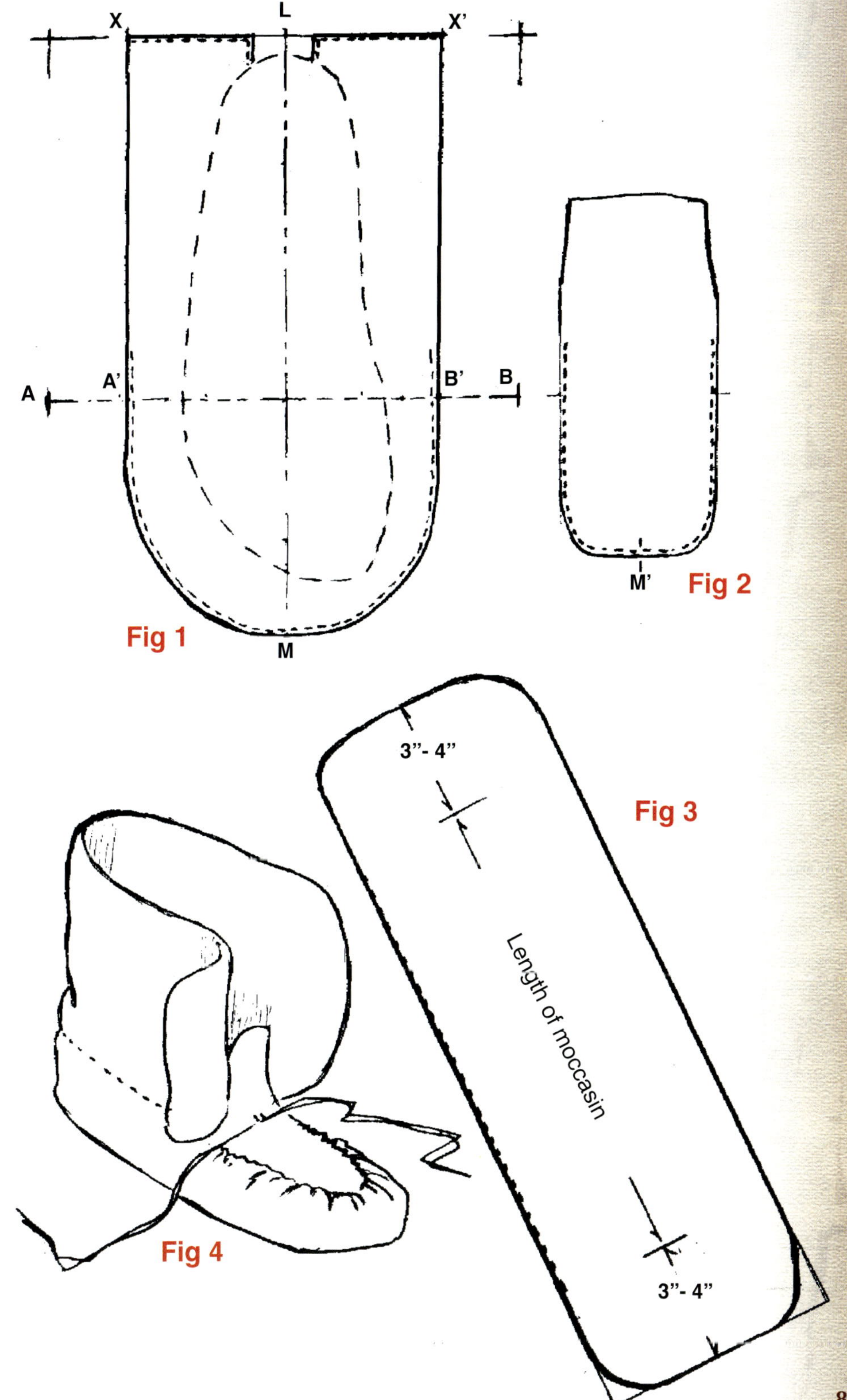
X
L
X'
A
A'
B'
B
M
Fig 1
M'
Fig 2
3"- 4"
Fig 3
Length of moccasin
3"- 4"
Fig 4

Yukon
Boot Top

1. See General Instructions.
2. A B = circumference.
3. A' B' + insert-tongue = **A B** (**Fig. 1** and **2**).
4. L M is leather length with allowance at heel (1/2" to 3/4") under foot to base of big toe nail. (See **Fig. G-3A**, page 21).
5. This moccasin is suited to heavy leather such as moose or elk. Heavy leather usually means wider spacing in stitching.
6. Attach "insert tongue" to sole and sew to point **A'** or **B'**. Use wider stitch but keep a 2 to 1 ratio so as to "gather" the sole piece to the insert.
7. The foot opening is a bit larger for this pattern. (More than 1/2 the length of moccasin.)
8. Heel is sewn from **X X'** to **L**.
9. The heel tab is tacked with a few stitches on outside. See Heel Details on page 24.
10. See **Fig. 4** and **3**. The boot top may be 8". The length or circumference can be found by careful measuring of foot opening.
11. Start at heel seam (See **Fig. 3**) and sew around foot opening, then up the back.
12. This is a bit difficult sewing, but it can be done and the resulting seam will be inside.
13. Note location of tie string on this pattern. This, being a snow moccasin, has as few holds as possible. See General Instructions for making holes for ties.

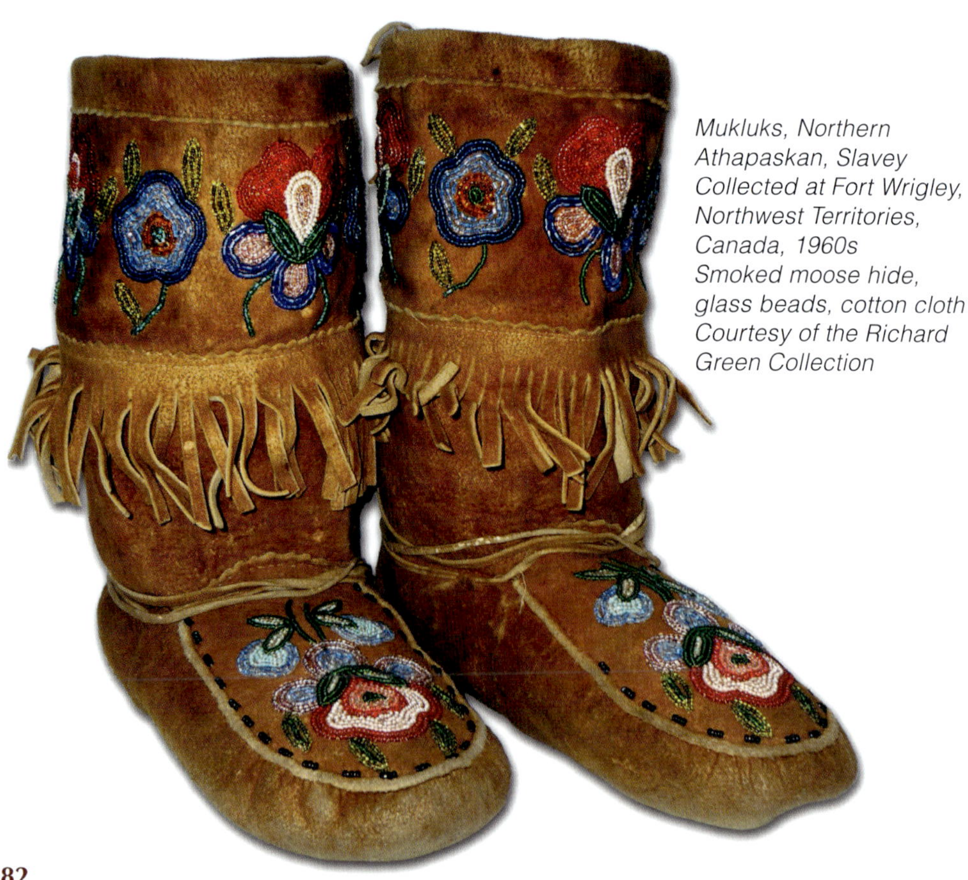

Mukluks, Northern Athapaskan, Slavey
Collected at Fort Wrigley, Northwest Territories, Canada, 1960s
Smoked moose hide, glass beads, cotton cloth
Courtesy of the Richard Green Collection

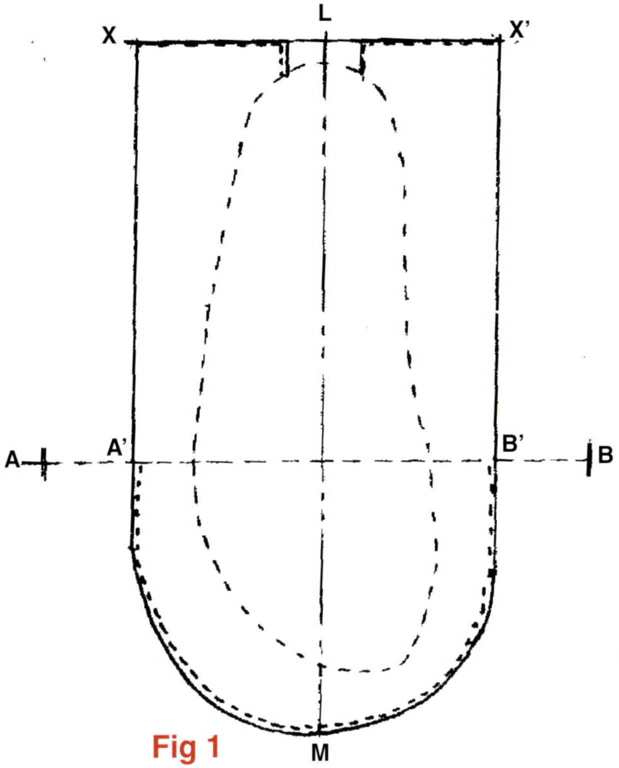

L

X X'

A A' B' B

M

Fig 1

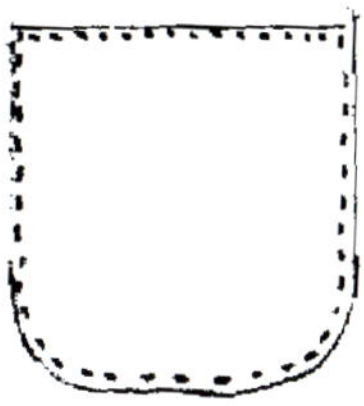

Fig 2

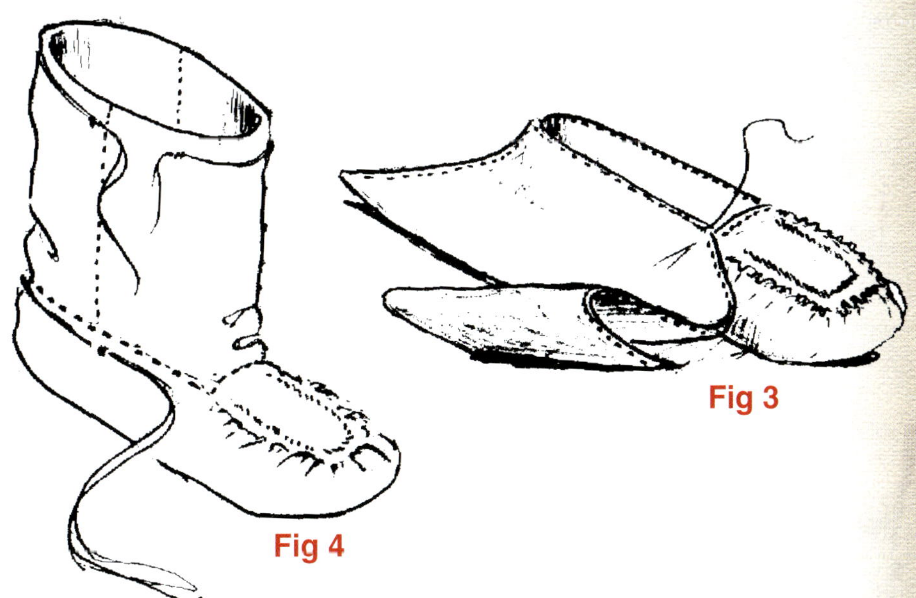

Fig 4

Fig 3

Mukluk

Gatherd Toe and Heel - Shaped Sole

Mukluks, or Kamik, are a soft boot traditionally made of reindeer hide or seal skin and were originally worn by the aboriginal people of the Arctic, including the Inuit and Yupik. The term mukluk is often used for any soft boot designed for cold weather. The word "mukluk" is of Yupik origin, from maklak, the bearded seal, while "kamik" is an Inuit word. Designed for wear in cold climates, mukluks are light in weight, allowing hunters to move very quietly. They can be decorated with beads and pompoms and are often lined with soft furs of small animals such as fox, rabbit and raccoon.

1. See General Instructions.
2. Determine **A' B'** by measuring foot (at line **A B**) about 3/4" above the floor.
3. **A' B'** plus vamp (See **Fig. 3**) must equal circumference. Note that line **A' B'** is point to measure and that points **Y** and **Z** are midway or 1/2 length of shaped sole. Add 1/2" to **A B** measurement as this is loose fitting.
4. The curve **A' M B'** is just slightly smaller than the foot outline around the toes. If the curve is made symmetrically the pattern may be used for both Mukluk. See **Fig. 3**.
5. The "gathering" at toe and heel must pull the leather in to foot size.
6. The best "gathering" is done by dampening the toe and heel. Be sure not to get it too damp or the leather will swell and make the gathering more difficult.
7. Use a strong nylon or linen thread and as small a strtch as possible, 1/8" weave the thread in and out, such as in (**Fig. 1** on page 17).
8. Tie off one end of the thread and work in the creases or folds. Work the folds several times if need be before tying off thread. Do the same with the heel. Work the folds at both toe and heels until the right size is obtained, then tie off both gathering threads.
9. Center vamp piece (See **Fig. 3**) over shaped sole. See if points **Y** and **Z** reach the midpoint on shaped sole piece. If the two pieces match, start sewing.
10. Start sewing at point **M** (right side out) catch every fold with a "whip stitch". See stitch sheet, pages 26 and 27. Sew to point **Y** or **Z** and tie off. Start at **M** again and sew other side.
11. The boot tops are sewn on next. Measure from **Z** to around heel to **Y**. This gives length of top piece. See **Fig. 3**. (Note that **K Y** and **K Z** are same length as shown in **Fig. 3** as **Z L**. **Z L Y** on **Fig. 4** must be same length as sole from **Z L Y** in **Fig. 1.**.
12. Sew front first from **K** to **Z**, then **K** to **Y**. (See **Fig. 44**) Sew from **Z** to **Y** around the heel. (Right side out).
13. Be sure to sew in tie strips. These slope to the rear as they cross around the heel and tie in front at the ankle.

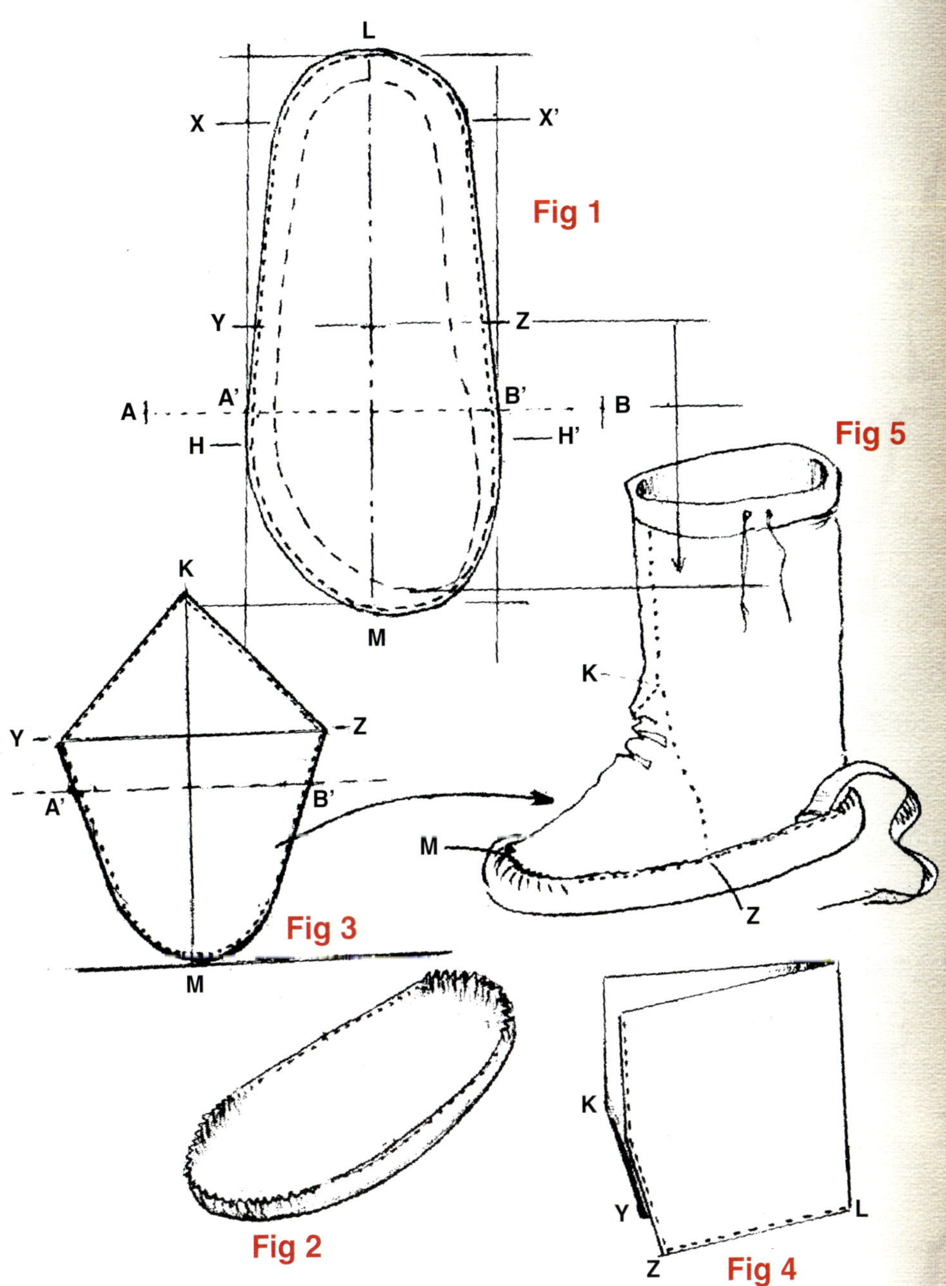
L
X
X'
Fig 1
Y
Z
A
A'
B'
B
H
H'
M
Fig 5
K
Y
Z
A'
B'
K
M
Z
Fig 3
M
Fig 2
K
Y
L
Z
Fig 4

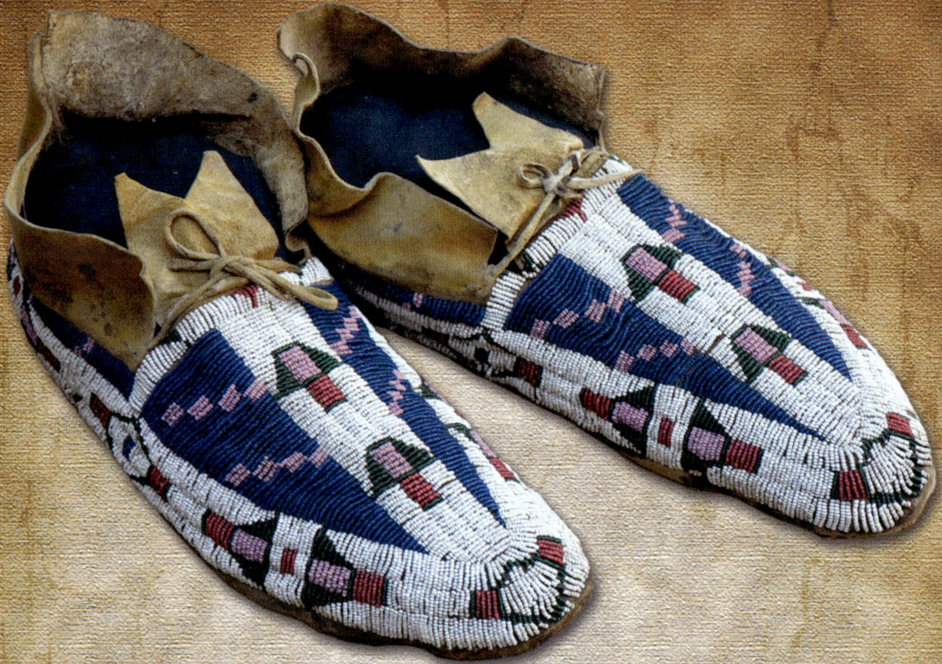

Cheyenne Man's Moccasins, circa 1870-1880. *Native tanned hide with rawhide soles, fully beaded in classic 19th century designs and colors. Private Collection.*

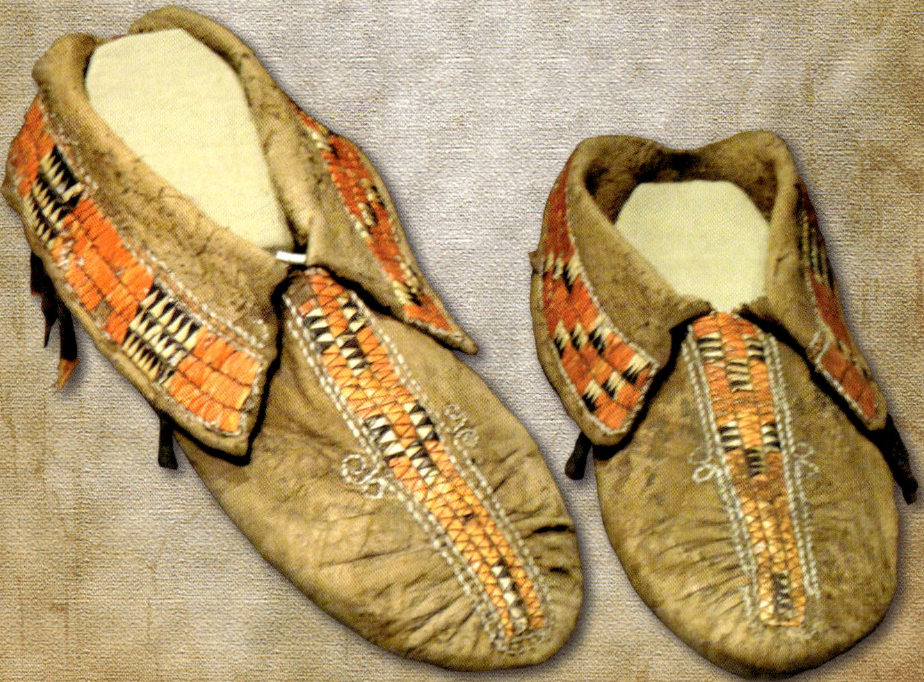

Eastern Woodlands Moccasins of the late 18th or early 19th century. *With dyed porcupine quill decoration along the edges of the side flaps and covering the seam of the vamp. Staatliches Museum für Völkerkunde - München*

References & Web Links

Many excellent books with full color photographs and identification of footwear are available, as well as hundreds of excellent, on-line photographs from some of the major museums housing large collections of American Indian material. Some of the best ones are listed here but diligent internet searches will reveal many more. However, a word of caution is advisable, as many times tribal attributions were assigned by museums and collectors based on the tribe from which an item was collected. Due to trading, gifting and intermarriage, these are not always correct.

Books:

A Persistent Vision - Richard Conn
American Indian Art - Norman Feder
Blackfeet Crafts - John C. Ewers
Circles of the World - Richard Conn
Crow Indian Beadwork - William Wildschutt and John C. Ewers
Footsteps on the Sacred Earth: Southwestern Collection of The Bata Shoe Museum - Jill Oakes & Rick Riewe
Hau Kola! - Barbara Hail
Pride of the Indian Wardrobe; Northern Athapaskan Footwear - Judy Thompson
Quill and Beadwork of the Western Sioux - Carrie Lyford
Splendid Heritage: Perspectives on American Indian Art - John & Marva Warnock, Editors
http://www.splendidheritage.com/SplendidHeritage.pdf
The Arapaho - Alfred Kroeber

Museums:

American Museum of Natural History (AMNH) - Washington, D.C.
http://www.amnh.org/exhibitions/permanent-exhibitions/
http://anthro.amnh.org/north
Bata Shoe Museum - Toronto Canada
http://www.allaboutshoes.ca/en/
Denver Art Museum - Denver, Colorado
http://www.denverartmuseum.org/
National Museum of the American Indian (NMAI) - Washington, D.C.
http://www.americanindian.si.edu/searchcollections/results.aspx?regid=341&sort=1
Smithsonian Institution - Washington, D.C.
http://www.si.edu/Museums/american-indian-museum

Magazines:

American Indian Crafts & Culture Magazine - Published by Tyrone Stewart, Tulsa, Oklahoma
Moccasin Tracks - Published by the California Indian Hobbyist Association
Whispering Wind Magazine - Published by Written Heritage, Folsom, Louisiana
http://www.writtenheritage.com/

Website Links:

American Museum of Natural History
http://anthro.amnh.org/anthropology/databases/north_public/north_public.htm
Arapaho Moccasins from the Museum & Research Center of the American Mountain Men
http://user.xmission.com/~drudy/mtman/html/skchbk02.html
Braintanning - www.braintan.com
Detroit Historical Society http://detroiths.pastperfect-online.com/33029cgi/mweb.exe?request=keyword;keyword=moccasin; dtype=d
Heritage Auctions - www.HA.com
Infinity of Nations Exhibit -National Museum of the American Indian - New York, NY.
http://nmai.si.edu/exhibitions/infinityof nations/introduction.htm
Native American Technology and Art
http://www.nativetech.org/clothing/moccasin/detail/ute.html
Splendid Heritage (Moccasins & Clothing)
http://www.splendidheritage.com/SplendidHeritage.pdf

About the Author

George M. White - Artist, Craftsman, Teacher

George was born in Nebraska in 1912. At the age of two, his family moved to eastern Montana, one of many families lured West in search of free land an opportunity. The prairie, pristine and vast, was, however, reluctant to share its gifts, save its abundance of sticky red "gumbo" which clung fiercely to the feet of man and beast, making farming nearly impossible. Taming this land was not easy, and, after a couple of disappointing years, many homesteaders left their sod homes and tar paper shacks and moved into "town".

Likewise, George's father, "Doc White", a dentist, eventually moved his family into Lewistown. As a young man, George spent a lot of time exploring the hills and mountains around Lewistown on foot and on horseback. Undoubtedly this prepared him for a lifelong interest in and appreciation of the Native American culture, especially its spiritual beliefs, social values, music, and hand crafts.

Although George lost vision in one eye in a childhood accident, he was gifted in "seeing" things through the eyes of an artist, geologist and archeologist. He had the unusual ability, an intuitive sense, of how things were 100, 200, or 3,000 years ago. He demonstrated this by locating unrecorded buffalo jumps, sacred circles, and encampments through out Montana.

He not only "saw" things as they were but had the manual dexterity to replicate a wide variety of handcrafted items such as: moccasins, snowshoes, baskets, beadwork, and more. His keen insight and appreciation of the Native American culture, its artisans, and handcrafts is recorded in the many craft manuals that he has written and illustrated. George was a master carver and sculptor, and his bronze work depicts Native American activities as well as wild animals and horses.

George exalted the human hand and its ability to manipulate its environment. He stated that it is the human hand that shaped history and put man on the moon.